MAKING SENSE

MAKING SENSE

Small-Group Comprehension Lessons for English Language Learners

K–8

Juli Kendall & Outey Khuon

Whittier Elementary School
Long Beach Unified School District
Long Beach, CA

Stenhouse Publishers
Portland, Maine

Stenhouse Publishers
www.stenhouse.com

Credits

Pages 83, 93, 108, 277, 282: from *Strategies That Work: Teaching Comprehension to Enhance Understanding* by Stephanie Harvey and Anne Goudvis. Copyright © 2000. Reprinted by permission Stenhouse Publishers.

Pages 101, 103, 116: from *Words, Words, Words: Teaching Vocabulary in Grades 4–12* by Janet Allen. Copyright © 1999. Reprinted by permission Stenhouse Publishers.

Judge Rabbit and the Snail Race reprinted by permission Jimmy R. Suon.

Library of Congress Cataloging-in-Publication Data

Kendall, Juli, 1949–
    Making Sense : small-group comprehension lessons for English language learners / Juli Kendall and Outey Khuon.
        p. cm.
    Includes bibliographical references and index.
    ISBN 1-57110-409-7 (alk. paper)
    1. English language—Study and teaching—Foreign speakers. 2. Group work in education. 3. Small groups. I. Khuon, Outey, 1950–. II. Title.

PE1128.A2K415 2005
428'.0071—dc22

Manufactured in the United States of America on acid-free paper
10 09 08 07 06 05 9 8 7 6 5 4 3 2 1

For the children

Contents

Acknowledgments

In many ways we have been writing this book for the last fifteen years but just didn't know it. It took Philippa Stratton, visiting our school and observing our teaching, to help us see it. She has been with us since the beginning of this project as we had Cambodian noodle soup, Chinese fried bread, and Thai coffee together at La Lune, in Long Beach. Who could have known that she would discover Frederick Lipp, the author of *The Caged Birds of Phnom Penh* and *Bread Song,* living in Portland, Maine? It truly is a small world.

We are indebted to many teachers who shared their expertise with us, especially Wendy Wahlen, Puthea Ing, Jason Cordero, Chansorado Chum, Linaromy Prom, Anita Gomez, Walter Yang, Chris Langemo, Lee Neubauer, Joan Shifflett, and Mory Ouk. All of them welcomed us into their classrooms and shared their students with us. To these teachers we say, You know what is important for English Language Learners, and you make sure that all your students are prepared for the years ahead. Thank you for all you do.

Dr. Wayne Wright from the University of Texas, San Antonio, College of Education and Human Development, Division of Bicultural-Bilingual Studies, read an overview of our writing and gave us valuable suggestions. Thanks, Wayne!

Special thanks to Stenhouse Publishers. You really know your stuff! You got us going, believed in us, kept us going, helped us sound and look our best, and got the word out. Three cheers for Philippa Stratton, Jay Kilburn, Doug Kolmar, and everyone else!

I (Outey) am indebted to my former principals, Dr. Randy Ward and Mary Marquez, who believed in me as I became a teacher for the second time and provided me with endless, valuable support. Without their encouragement, I would not be working as a teacher in the United States today. I am also indebted to my friends Alejandro Morales, David Taylor, Sharon Lazo-Nakamoto, and Paul Boyd Batstone, who never refused me when I needed their help. Last, but not least, I wish to thank my husband, Vandy, who in his own traditional Cambodian way supports my work with love and patience.

I (Juli) am indebted to Judy Swanson, who included me in her research and asked me hard, probing questions that caused me to become more reflective about my teaching, and continues to be my friend. I also wish to express my appreciation to my first editor, John Norton, of MiddleWeb http://www.middleweb.com and Teacher Leaders Network http://www.teacherleaders.org

fame. He told me several years ago, "I think you should write a book," and put me in touch with Stenhouse Publishers. I owe him additionally because as we worked on chapters 4 and 5, we drew on the reading/writing journals he so skillfully edited for MiddleWeb. A few of the lessons in chapters 3 and 4 first saw the light of day in the MiddleWeb journals. Thank you, John.

Undoubtedly, this book would not have been possible without the love and support of my husband, Jim. His ability to brainstorm big ideas is inspiring. He patiently coaches me on how to take pictures that tell a story, and he easily solves each and every technological issue that comes along. Jim, you are truly amazing!

Together we wish to thank all the students with whom we have worked over the years in Cambodia and in the United States. They teach us that it is the children who show us what they need and where to go next. Follow the child!

INTRODUCTION

Introduction (Setting the Scene and Introducing Ourselves)

Sometimes life's circumstances lead us in new directions. We met during 1989 and 1990 as we worked with a grant from the U.S. Department of Education for Khmer-speaking (Cambodian) students in Long Beach. Our collaboration consisted of lots of demonstration lessons of English language development strategies and modeling primary language support using the Preview-Review strategy. On classroom days we hauled a luggage cart overflowing with wonderful books, pictures, and other forms of realia for use with whole-class and small-group instruction.

We frequently heard, "That's nice, but how can I teach these kids to read? They don't know English."

In a perfect world, all students would come to school with a strong foundation in English, but that's not the case. Our underlying belief, however, is that all students are capable of learning English as they learn to read with understanding, given the proper support, appropriate instruction, and time. It's easy to see how this could look overwhelming to a teacher faced with a classroom full of students, some of whom speak English and some of whom don't. Not only that, but frequently, students learning English are at different levels. Several might be just beginning to speak the language, whereas others might need more help with academic language in content areas. Reading

figure 1.1 *(above left) Juli uses charts and notebooks to help students use strategies.*

figure 1.2 *(above right) Outey reads a big book to a small group of English language learners.*

teachers need to learn how to coordinate instruction for all these different language levels. Teaching everyone the same thing, all at the same time, all day long, just doesn't seem to work.

Small-group strategy lessons: that's the solution we found to teaching reading comprehension strategies to English Language Learners. This book is about how to make that happen in your classroom. But all the work we do, as Lucy Calkins says, "stands on the shoulders" of others. Many of the ideas, terms, and forms we have used and adapted are extensions of the work of others. For instance, the idea of using a synthesizing frame to scaffold students' thinking about their reading came to us as we read Debbie Miller's chapter on synthesizing in *Reading with Meaning,* and the headings in the vocabulary inference chart (figure 3.6) are the same as those in Debbie's chart. The FQR chart in Chapter 5 is from *Strategies That Work* by Stephanie Harvey and Anne Goudvis and the idea of wonder poems comes from Cris Tovani in her chapter "What Do You Wonder?" from *I Read It But I Don't Get It.*

The groundbreaking work of these Denver-area Public Education and Business Coalition thinkers has helped us understand the role of comprehension in the teaching of reading as we have collaborated to find ways to build background knowledge and develop content literacy for English Language Learners. They have forged a path by leading our thinking about how to teach comprehension in new and exciting directions. Undoubtedly, this book would not be possible without their trail blazing. Many teachers of English Language Learners have struggled with strategy instruction, and building on others' comprehension work, we have developed these lessons so students can use strategies in their reading as their oral language develops.

In addition, we borrowed the language of mini-lesson terms from the Architecture of Mini-lessons. We learned this language through the Teachers College Reading and Writing Institutes we attended. Mark Hardy, Isoke Nia, and Kathleen Tolan guided us as we implemented this four-part architecture. It ensures that our students have the necessary background experiences to understand our lessons, receive new information, be actively involved in the learning, and have opportunities to apply strategies.

Since our collaboration in the federal grant for English Language Learners, we have worked as literacy specialists and reading teachers in elementary and middle school across grades K–8. During this time, we have learned that when it comes to finding ways to differentiate reading strategy instruction for English Language Learners, many teachers struggle with how to organize their classrooms to provide this instruction for students at different levels of English. All across the country, teachers grapple with the same issues: How will I provide strategy instruction for my students who are at different levels of English? What are some ways I can organize my classroom so all students can participate fully in reading with meaning? Finding satisfactory answers to these questions is challenging, given the constraints of current educational guidelines. But there are some simple solutions that work.

After school, a group of fourth- and fifth-grade teachers were discussing how to teach comprehension strategies to their students, 90 percent of whom are English Language Learners. "Why is it so hard for kids to get the strategies?" one teacher asked. "I teach them to the whole class and we use them with different stories and we come back to them again and again, but the kids just don't get it."

"It might be that, as English Language Learners, the kids need more teaching and modeling of reading comprehension strategies," another teacher responded. "If you used some of the time during workshop to do small-group strategy instruction with kids who are at the same level of English proficiency, it might target their needs."

"Well, maybe I'll give it a try," the first teacher decided. "But you know how my kids act during workshop time. They are all over the place."

This book takes the position that oral language development and reading comprehension strategy instruction can go hand in hand. By using small groups to provide support, teachers use their knowledge about how language is learned to scaffold instruction as they teach reading comprehension strategies.

Learning to comprehend text for English Language Learners complements language learning since oral language is the foundation of reading and writing. But it does not necessarily match oral language proficiency. Beginning speakers may be able to use prior knowledge and background experience (schema theory) to understand simple stories and yet not be able to discuss them. In the same regard, advanced students may discuss making connections to their reading and ask questions, and still need academic vocabulary development to comprehend content-area text. At every English language level there are ways to draw students into reading with understanding using comprehension strategies. But questions abound.

What oral language ability does a student at the beginning stages of English proficiency need to use prior knowledge to make connections to text? How do students at the intermediate stage ask questions about their reading and learn to infer? What are some ways to teach students at the advanced stage to synthesize during reading? What are the criteria for selecting text? How can you assess students' use of strategies? What do you do if they don't get it?

Using Small Groups for Strategy Instruction

Our work in classrooms and across grade levels suggests that teachers most often provide students strategy instruction in whole-class settings. Many teachers organize whole-class mini-lessons and expect that their students will learn how to use reading comprehension strategies from them. Although many students do learn in whole-class settings, some need a more intimate setting in which teachers provide additional modeling of strategy use and students feel comfortable practicing the strategies and receiving feedback. This is often the case for English Language Learners.

In many classrooms the emphasis is on constructing strategy lessons, and often the scaffolding of the teaching gets less attention. It's very easy to get caught up in highlighters, sticky notes, and two-column charts while overlooking grouping structures.

In addition, small-group strategy instruction for English Language Learners can look like a complicated process. It involves knowing how to teach reading comprehension strategies, recognizing stages of language proficiency in a variety of students, and finding the most effective ways to deliver the instruction. Once classroom management is in place, small-group instruction provides an ideal setting for students learning English.

English Language Learners benefit from small-group strategy instruction for many reasons. Here are a few:

Low-anxiety environment
Opportunities for teacher-to-student interactions
Guided student-to-student interactions
More on-task behaviors
Easier to check for understanding
Facilitates monitoring and adjusting instruction

How This Book Is Organized

This book about small-group strategy instruction gives explicit and concrete ways to teach students reading comprehension strategies as they learn English. We suggest that lessons begin once students are familiar with school routines and are comfortable with the teacher and each other.

These strategy lessons are part of a comprehensive literacy program. They are not a complete program by themselves. What makes them effective is the classroom environment that teachers create to support English Language Learners. The next section, "The Nuts and Bolts of Small-Group Strategy Instruction for English Language Learners," explains how to create the conditions to make this work.

The strategy lessons are divided into five sections based on English language proficiency:

- Preproduction lessons
- Early Production lessons
- Speech Emergence lessons
- Intermediate Fluency lessons
- Advanced Fluency lessons

The instructional materials (books, charts, notebooks, and so on) listed in these lessons may often be used with students with more or less language proficiency. Because every student's needs are different, always check for understanding to make sure the materials are comprehensible and support oral language development.

Within each section, the lessons are further divided by comprehension strategies.

- Making Connections (Using Prior Knowledge to Make Connections to Text)
- Asking Questions
- Visualizing (Making Pictures in Your Mind)
- Inferring (Reading Between the Lines)
- Determining Importance in Nonfiction and Informational Text (not in Beginning stages)
- Synthesizing Information (not in Beginning stages)

Each of the five sections begins with a vignette of younger students' learning strategies, along with lessons for teaching strategies and a book list of possible anchor texts (Harvey and Goudvis 2000). In addition, there is a section on older students at that particular stage of language proficiency that includes a vignette about students, strategy lessons, and a list of books.

These small-group strategy lessons come from our experience teaching reading comprehension strategies to English Language Learners. For the last four years we've collaborated daily, with improving reading comprehension the focus of our work.

Each small-group strategy lesson includes two sections: Instructional Materials and Teaching Moves.

Instructional Materials (what makes the lesson comprehensible)

- Resources (realia such as concrete objects, photographs, illustrations, student work, music, video, technology, and field trips)
- Books
- Materials (such as pencils and pens, paper, markers, sticky notes, charts, graphic organizers, bookmarks, and strategy application notebooks)

Teaching Moves (what the lesson looks like)

- Start-up/Connection (helping students develop background experience and use prior knowledge to connect to the lesson)
- Give Information (telling students what they are going to learn, why they are learning it, and then teaching them)
- Active Involvement (often occurs during the teaching as students practice what they are learning while the teacher checks for understanding and monitors and adjusts instruction)
- Off You Go (opportunities for students to practice what they learned with peers or independently)

The small-group strategy lessons in this book give an indication of what English Language Learners can learn about reading comprehension as they progress through the stages of language proficiency. We made decisions about what lessons to include based on how students responded. We picked lessons that motivated students by actively engaging them in strategy use.

Not all of these lessons will be necessary for your students. As you work through the book, keep in mind the standards for which you are responsible and choose those lessons that match your students' needs.

The Nuts and Bolts of Small-Group Strategy Instruction for English Language Learners

There is no silver bullet for teaching English Language Learners. Language proficiency is a moving target, and each year in school the linguistic demands are greater.

Imagine chasing after a bus as it pulls away from the curb, running and running to try to catch up only to be left standing in exhaust fumes as it rumbles away. Or visualize Harry Potter. He's in the midst of a Quidditch match. Flying on his broomstick, he swoops down to catch the nearly invisible Snitch only to watch as it darts off in another direction.

Kids learning English often find themselves in similar situations. It's a fact: a third grader needs to be able to comprehend more than a second grader. Sixth graders need to learn about ancient civilizations while they are learning to read in English. As language skills increase, the expectations do, too.

The strategy lessons in this book are kid tested, but they won't help students hit the bull's eye unless their classrooms support them as they use the strategies they are learning. Based on our experience, certain conditions need to be in place in classrooms to support small-group strategy instruction for English Language Learners. Among these are flexible, data-driven grouping structures, supportive teaching environments, well-organized classroom management, and an understanding of the stages of language proficiency.

Grouping Structures—Data-Driven Instruction with Flexible Grouping

One of the first considerations with small-group instruction is identifying which students will work together. Flexible groups based on students' needs provide opportunities for students to have targeted instruction for a short period of time. Often, groups are formed just for particular students who are struggling with a specific strategy, such as asking questions. That means the groups do not always consist of the same students, as used to be the case, with the "bluebird group" being the low reading group.

With strategy instruction, groups are formed based on data. Students are assessed in a variety of ways to determine what they know about using strategies as they read. Then instruction is planned based on the assessment results. After the instruction, students are assessed again and groups are reconfigured based upon their instructional needs. It is this ongoing cycle—assessing, planning instruction, learning, and assessing again to plan the next instructional steps and regroup students—that provides a flexible structure for grouping students. Small groups are not formed based on ability but rather are data driven, and students are frequently regrouped based on assessments.

One of the assessments used to form small groups of English Language Learners is the student's stage of language proficiency. This information helps teachers select books that provide the right balance of support and challenge and allows them to promote oral language development. Often small groups of English Language Learners may be mixed across stages of language proficiency because of other assessment data or numbers of students. In this case, it is important to provide plenty of comprehensible input (such as pictures, realia, and hands-on activities) and scaffolding to make sure all students in the group have access to the lessons and comprehend the instruction.

While teachers are working with students in a small group, there's always the question, What are the others in the classroom doing? Providing high-quality activities that engage the rest of the class in literacy learning is an important consideration with small-group instruction. Debbie Diller has written two books that provide solutions for this dilemma. *Literacy Work Stations* includes activities appropriate for primary students, and her new book *Practice with Purpose: Literary Work Stations for Grades 3–6* adds activities for the intermediate grades. Many of these ideas are also appropriate for English Language Learners.

Teaching Environments

A variety of teaching environments can support small-group instruction. We've worked in three different configurations plus after-school tutoring.

Workshops in Regular Class Settings

The whole class participates in a variety of independent activities designed to enhance instruction while the teacher works with a small group for strategy instruction. Usually, the teacher has previously done mini-lessons with the whole class to teach the strategy and wants to do additional teaching and follow-up, targeting English Language Learners. Students who are not in the small group frequently do independent reading as part of their workshop activities. In some instances, an additional teacher works in the classroom in coordination with the classroom teacher during this time.

Flexible Grouping (Centers, Rotations, Work Stations)

The whole class is divided into flexible groups based on certain criteria. The criteria change based on instructional needs, so the students in the groups are frequently changing as well. One purpose for grouping is to provide strategy instruction that matches the stage of language proficiency of English Language Learners. Students participate in one to four different groups each day, depending on the class format. Most often our groups include as many as five students. We find that more than five in a group restricts the amount of conversation and learning that takes place. We usually choose our groups based on the stage of language proficiency and strategy assessments. Groups often span more than one stage. In that case, it is important to be flexible and carefully observe how students comprehend the lessons so we can adjust instruction.

Pull-out Classes

Students leave their classrooms to participate in small-group strategy instruction with a "pull-out" teacher. Often this teacher works with programs for Title 1 and/or English Language Learners. Will these lessons work on their own, isolated from classroom contexts? A skilled teacher in a pull-out setting such as ELD, ESOL, or ESL can make these lessons work. However, constant communication with the classroom teacher facilitates students' integration of strategies into classroom activities.

Classroom Management

It won't matter how wonderful the small-group strategy lessons are or how much time the teacher spends planning if classroom management to support small-group instruction is not in place. Remember the teacher who said, "But you know how my kids act during workshop time. They are all over the place." Small-group instruction works only when classroom routines support independence.

Expectations and Standards for Behavior

To set the expectations and standards for behavior during small-group instruction, we use three simple guidelines, posted on a large wall chart.

Expectations and Standards for Behavior

1. Respect everyone.
2. Follow directions.
3. Ask three, then me.

We teach students each of these expectations as part of our initial whole-group instruction. Number one—Respect everyone—refers to how we all wish to be treated. Number two—Follow directions—reinforces the importance of listening carefully and paying attention. Number three—Ask three, then me—follows up on the idea that students need to take responsibility for their own learning. Before asking the teacher a question, without disrupting instruction, they ask three students. If none of the students' responses meets their needs, they can ask the teacher. This limits interruptions during small-group instruction as well as teaching a strategy for developing independence as a learner. Additionally, it helps the teacher monitor what students understand about their assignments. If three other students cannot satisfactorily answer the student's question, the information probably needs to be restated to the whole group.

To teach these expectations we discuss each one separately, asking the students to think about what it means and then to draw an illustration of what it looks like. Each student shares his or her work with a small group and keeps the illustration in a notebook to refer to from time to time. Just like we teach each strategy, we carefully teach each of these expectations so that we can hold students accountable for their behavior.

Teaching the Desired Behaviors

We want our small-group strategy instruction to go smoothly, so we keep interruptions to a minimum. When we teach other students in the classroom to work independently as we teach a small group, they accept more responsibility for their learning. To facilitate a gradual release of responsibility to the students, we begin by having all students do the same activity before we even start working with small groups.

For example, we want all students in our classrooms to participate in independent reading. Before we start small-group instruction, we teach them how to do this. We give them a rubric by which to judge their independent reading.

Independent Reading Rubric

1. **Oops!** I wasted precious reading time.
2. **So-so . . .** I read some of the time. I used strategies to help me understand what I was reading.
3. **Good!** I read most of the time. I used strategies to help me understand what I was reading.
4. **Wow!** I read the whole time. I used strategies to help me understand what I was reading.

Adapted from a photograph in *The Art of Teaching Reading* (Calkins 2001)

After a whole-class discussion of the criteria from the rubric, everyone reads independently for a set period of time, usually fifteen to thirty minutes, and then evaluates their reading based on the rubric. This self-evaluation has a profound effect on students' behavior during independent reading. They can easily see where they fall on the rubric and what they need to do to improve.

After we teach independent reading using the rubric, we choose a small group of students for strategy instruction. The rest of the students are reading independently following the rubric and the Expectations and Standards for Behavior that are posted on a large wall chart. Students keep track of their rubric scores for independent reading as a self-assessment and write a reflection once a month. Teaching independent reading to the whole group before starting small-group instruction provides an activity that engages students in applying strategies and gradually releases responsibility to them while the teacher works with small groups.

Stages of Language Proficiency

Adapted from Krashen (1996) *and* NWREL (2003)

This table provides an overview of what teachers can expect from students at each stage of language proficiency and how they can use that information to plan instruction.

Stages of Language Proficiency	Student Characteristics	How Students Demonstrate Understanding	Implications for Planning Instruction
Preproduction (Silent Period)	Student listens and responds nonverbally by performing actions, gesturing, nodding, shaking head, touching, pointing, and drawing. Students are not expected to talk; "silent period." Students are taking in new language and trying to make sense of it to meet basic needs.	Listen, draw, move, select, mime, choose, act/act out, circle, match pictures or facts, lineups, role playing, demonstration, pantomime, illustrating, illustrating vocabulary, pointing to pictures for an answer.	Provide activities geared to tap their knowledge, but do not force production (speaking). Total Physical Response is effective as a teaching strategy. Often students can comprehend much more than they can produce. Lessons are centered on listening comprehension and building receptive vocabulary. Students understand language that has been made comprehensible through pictures, realia, hands-on activities, etc.
Early Production	Students begin to respond with brief answers in one- or two-word phrases. Students have a small, active vocabulary. Errors in grammar and pronunciation are frequent.	Name, list, label, categorize, group, tell/say, respond, answer (with one/two words), cut and paste, draw and remember, draw and describe, Concentration-type games, demonstration, pantomime, illustration, charades, role playing.	Teaching strategies consist of extending listening skills and asking questions that will elicit yes/no, choice, one- or two-word responses, or even sentence completion. It is important that students be able to take risks and experiment with new language in a low-anxiety setting. Lessons at this stage expand receptive vocabulary, and classroom activities encourage students to produce vocabulary they already understand.

Stages of Language Proficiency	Student Characteristics	How Students Demonstrate Understanding	Implications for Planning Instruction
			Students demonstrate comprehension of material by giving short responses to easy yes/no questions and either/or questions.
			They can also respond to simple who, what, when, where questions.
Speech Emergence	Students use language to communicate more freely and begin to use English for academic purposes. There is a noticeable increase in listening comprehension. Students will try to speak in short phrases.	Recall, summarize, retell, describe, define, role play, explain, restate, categorize, preference ranking, games, cause/effect, compare/contrast, sequence, discussion, prediction.	Opportunities for students to interact with each other and negotiate for meaning are critical at this stage. Lessons continue to expand students' vocabulary, and class activities are designed to encourage higher, more complex levels of language use. Ask students how-and-why questions that elicit short responses. They will be able to participate in many of the mainstream academic subjects.
Intermediate Fluency	Students engage in conversation and produce connected narrative. They express their ideas comprehensibly in both oral and written communication. Students conduct conversations in English that are approaching native fluency.	Analyze, evaluate, create, justify, defend, support, debate, examine, complete, describe in detail, compare/contrast, cause/effect, predict. Questions: Who, did what, when, why, where?	Still developing academic competence, especially in the areas of reading and writing. As they continue to expand vocabulary, class activities are structured to develop higher levels of language use, incorporating reading and writing into content-area lessons. Ask open-ended questions to create opportunities for more complicated responses and use of complex sentences. Reading and writing activities: writing using frames, echo and choral reading, readers' theater, questioning.

Advanced Fluency Students at this stage demonstrate nativelike oral fluency but may have difficulty acquiring high levels of reading and writing. They often struggle with reading in content areas and need extensive content-area vocabulary development. It is important to include extensive, contextualized, academic vocabulary development. Include grade-level textbooks and other materials for content-area reading when selecting texts for strategy instruction.

Students at Each Stage of Proficiency

The following descriptions of students provide a real world, real time view of English Language Learners. They provide insight into what students are like at each stage of language proficiency. It is important to remember that students are individuals and will have some of the characteristics of a stage but not all. What is important about knowing a student's stage of language proficiency is that it facilitates instructional planning. It serves as a beginning assessment of what the student knows and is able to do. This information can then be used to plan appropriate instruction for English Language Learners that promotes oral language development and improves comprehension. To determine the stage of language proficiency for a student, read through the descriptions of the students and refer in the table to the section on student characteristics.

Voulach, five-year-old Cambodian girl: Preproduction

Voulach was not alone, surrounded by her three sisters and her father—always there for her to hide behind—when the offer of a snack stopped all her thoughts of hiding. Seated under the open-air ramada in the summer afternoon heat of the asphalt playground, she was eating from a paper container filled with Apple Jacks and milk.

She watched her sisters, checking frequently to see what her father was doing, and chewing quickly. Voulach finished her cereal. Snacks from the After School Program, that was what she'd been fascinated with. A simple question from the program coordinator, "Would you like a snack?" prompted her response, "Yes." Numerous other questions and prompts to speak were directed at her, encouraging her to say more. She remained silent.

"*Arkun,*" she said when she spoke again, her quiet "Thank you" in Khmer almost inaudible. Lowering her head, she carried her empty cereal box and milk carton to the trash can before scampering off with her family.

Mingmei, eleven-year-old Chinese girl: Preproduction

Five years of school in China, and Mingmei still appeared uncomfortable in a sixth-grade middle school class. It was because she spoke little English and comprehended even less. But really, she just needed a friend. Lacking oral communication skills, she had turned to a computerized translation device for comfort, typing frantically to make sense of what was happening around her. She needed to talk to someone, someone to answer her questions and help her work her way into the American school system.

Enter Chanlyda. Her class schedule changed and she came to sit in the chair across the table from Mingmei. Teachers knew she spoke Khmer, French, and English, but not Chinese. A sixth-grade girl who could have worked as a translator for the United Nations—how did Mingmei get so lucky! Somehow Chanlyda knew to start the conversation, and within minutes they were chattering away. She ate lunch with Mingmei every day and drew her into her circle of friends. As time passed, Mingmei put away her translation device, learned English quickly, and grew to love her school.

Holysun, six-year-old Cambodian boy: Early Production

He ran around the corner from the kindergarten play yard, passing his brother, Jarath, who was watering the gated-off garden, and chased by his third-grade sister, Yannary. "Holysun, stop!" she called as he headed off toward the board games on the playground. The responsibility of picking him up from his kindergarten class at the end of school fell to her.

In five minutes he was back, crying because someone had put green marker on his white uniform polo shirt. A moment later he was off again. "I do it later, I do it later!" the kindergartner yelled as his sister tried to call him back to the shaded picnic tables to start his homework.

Full of energy and glad to be finished with school for the day, he was happy just to be out on the playground running around. Enough with sitting still in class.

Radu, eleven-year-old Romanian boy: Early Production

It was Radu's attempts at trying to understand what kids were saying that had set him to thinking about the English lessons in school in Romania, and then suddenly to ask the teacher, "What do they mean? I didn't learn that in school in Romania." Listening attentively in class wasn't helping him understand the conversations of the students around him. There was no context for their conversation that he could comprehend.

"That's the bomb! I gotta get me some more," one girl commented. Radu just shook his head.

Even so, Radu's progress was amazing. In sixth grade he mastered the art of communicating with his peers. In seventh grade he mastered reading and writing in his content-area classes. By eighth-grade graduation, he was at the top of his class. Remarkable for just two and a half years.

Sophanny, seven-year-old Cambodian girl: Speech Emergence

With twinkling black eyes, a disarming smile, and a well-tuned sense of humor, Sophanny, the youngest of three sisters, demonstrated an incredible ability to read and write in English at an early age. She loved books and reading and doing homework. As she moved through first grade into second grade, each day seemed to bring a new discovery. There were exciting things to learn from books, amazing facts accumulated on field trips with her classmates, and a never-ending imagination. She used language to communicate freely about all her interests.

She also loved to dance, not just any dancing but Cambodian dances. Every Monday and Friday when the college student assistant came to the After School Program, she scampered up the steps. Eager to get started, she ran to the end of the hall with her friends and pulled off her shoes and socks. They worked for an hour to master hand moves, becoming more and more graceful as time passed. It was beautiful to watch these young children learning something special about their culture in the midst of their elementary school.

After dancing, Sophanny returned to her group of After School Program students to finish her homework. She used academic language as she worked on her math assignment. When her father came to pick her up, along with her younger brother and two older sisters, she waved a cheerful good-bye.

María, eleven-year-old Mexican girl: Speech Emergence

María was a mystery. Because she went back and forth between school in the United States and school in Mexico, her actual grade level was difficult to determine. At this point, she was in fifth grade. During the previous year she had developed a knack for writing using word processing. She had written poems, word-processed them, added graphics, and then printed copies for her teacher and her family. Technology was her favorite way to learn.

Now she was back again and ready for more. "When do we get to start using the computers?" she asked. "I want to do some research."

"Soon," Juli replied. "Once everyone has learned the rules about respecting our equipment."

During small-group time, Juli listened to her think aloud as she read through the book *Mice and Beans*. María loved the illustrations of the mice and found the grandmother's character endearing. "What do you like about this book?" Juli asked, trying to understand how to select other books María would enjoy.

"It's really funny," María told Juli. "I like funny books." Understanding the humor in what she was reading showed that her reading comprehension was improving.

Jefferson, nine-year-old Cambodian boy: Intermediate

Jefferson was a master at the game of checkers. The only problem was that the game set was missing all the black checkers. He wanted those for his game pieces, but instead he collected a set of blue and yellow plastic tiles to use in their place. He didn't seem to mind. "She's cheating!" he called out as the student assistant from the university moved her pieces on the checkerboard.

As well as being a game lover, he loved science. Several weeks later, he was carrying a plastic tub filled with dirt and leaves in from the playground. As he walked up the stairs to his class on the second floor, he announced, "Here comes a science experiment. Watch out!"

Questioned about why he was carrying a tub of dirt, he carefully explained. "This is a science experiment with dirt and water. First, we collect the dirt with stuff in it. Next, we pour water on top, and then we watch to see what happens and write down our observations." It was easy to see that this Cambodian fourth grader understood what he was going to do.

José, twelve-year-old Spanish-speaking boy: Intermediate

José was working on learning academic vocabulary. One thing that made this challenging is that while he was still working to master oral English, he was attempting to understand reading selections in content areas such as science. He was developing skill in content literacy by learning about the features of informational text. Using tables of contents, labels, italic, indexes, and diagrams, he had a developing understanding of how informational text is organized. In this way, the features of the text supported him as he learned new words and concepts. But sometimes it got confusing.

One day during a small-group strategy lesson, students were reading some informational text and answering the question "What is a glossary?" José seemed confused and commented, "It's like little stories that go through, and they…" At just the moment he was speaking, there was a loud announcement from the office, so he repeated his comments. "When they say that, I think it means that there's like holes and they go in."

To clear up his confusion, Juli clarified by saying, "So you are looking at the definitions of the words."

He answered, "Yes," and the group continued talking about the purpose of the glossary. The group decided a glossary was like a little dictionary with definitions for some of the important words and concepts in the book. As a result, José learned that a glossary is not just little stories but rather definitions of words. This was important because often when students misunderstand text it is because of this kind of confusion. Knowing how to use text features such as a glossary transfers to reading in other content areas.

Julie, eight-year-old Cambodian girl: Advanced

"Dreaming Is Believing," was the motto on Julie's T-shirt. It was perfect for her. Smart, cute, and chatty, this Cambodian third grader was full of life and interested in everything. But with such a sharp mind, it wasn't surprising that she also had lots of opinions to share. First on the list was her cousin who didn't like to play school with her. He obviously had other things he'd rather do. "Every day when I go to my older cousin's house, I ask her if we can play school," she said. "She teaches me everything that her teacher teaches her. She makes me books and stuff. We draw by ourselves. We're making books about our families. But her brother, my other cousin, doesn't like to play school with us. He doesn't like to listen to his sister. Sometimes he's not respectful."

Next on her list of things to talk about was her teacher, whom she loved. "My teacher is very nice," she said. "She is very respectful. If people are having a problem, we come to the rug and talk about it. She taught us that there is no tattle-taling. Well, really she taught us that we can only tattle on someone else if it solves a problem. We can't do it if it causes a problem."

She even had an opinion about her friends. "I have five girls who are my friends," she commented. "They are all respectful. But one of them, she is too hyper."

About her school, she said, "My school is good because it's really a respectful school."

The rest of us have plenty to learn from Julie.

Monique, thirteen-year-old Mexican girl: Advanced

Monique smiled as she came through Juli's sixth-grade classroom door in September. "I enrolled to be an eighth-grade student assistant," she said. "This is my elective class." She worked diligently all year long, helping struggling Spanish-speaking sixth graders make sense of writing workshop.

She entered the Lions Club Speech Contest in the spring even though many at school discouraged her. People were surprised when she won at this first level of competition. "She's been here only two years," they said.

She won the second level of competition two weeks later, and one of the eighth-grade students in the gifted and talented program said, "I could have done that, if I'd wanted to." She seemed confident and secure while she studied and practiced with her sixth-grade history teacher to prepare for the regional level.

After the contest, when she had been eliminated for exceeding the time limit, she reflected, "It was wonderful to get so far. So many people didn't think I should do it. But I knew I could."

Assessing Strategy Use for English Language Learners

Reading is all about understanding. The reason we teach strategies to kids is because, by using strategies as they read, their understanding and comprehension is enhanced. They make connections to the text. They ask questions and wonder. They create mental images and visualize by "making movies in their minds." They use background experience, prior knowledge, and comprehensible input to draw conclusions and inferences. They determine what is important in informational texts and content-area reading. They answer the question, "How has my thinking changed?" by synthesizing as they read. They constantly monitor their strategy use by asking the big question: Does it make sense? They do all this with the expectation that what they read will make sense.

But reading is an in-the-head behavior, invisible most of the time. So how can we assess students' use of strategies? There are a variety of ways to do so.

Standardized Tests The ultimate goal of strategy instruction is for kids to independently monitor their use of strategies as they read. Standardized test scores are one indication of whether or not kids "get it." Given a few reading selections in narrative and expository text, and a series of high-level multiple-choice questions, do they demonstrate that they understand what they are reading? Can they take what they have learned in class and practiced through independent reading, and apply it in this formal, structured situation?

Students' Conversations About Reading By listening in on students' conversations about books and other texts, teachers assess how well students understand what they read and how they are using strategies to help them comprehend text. Talking about texts also encourages the use of English for academic purposes, an important part of improving as a speaker of English. It also encourages students to self-assess how they use strategies.

Older Intermediate-Level Students Talk About Reading

Henry: "This book, *Mice and Beans*, it reminds me of Cinderella. I remember in the story there were mice that were helpful. Just like in this story. The mice help the lady. Sometimes mice are bad or good."

Veronica: "But it reminds me of another book I read, *If You Give a Mouse a Cookie*. We read that in first grade. But there's another one, *If You Give a Moose a Muffin*. They repeat over and over like this book."

Nestor: "Wait. It reminds me of when my sister was seven years old and we had a birthday party, and my mom bought a cake and I had to go to the store and get it on my bike, and I had to carry it all the way home. Just like the little old grandma who carries it all the way home in *Mice and Beans*."

Henry: "Did you fall off your bike?"

Nestor: "No. But I was scared."

Retellings (Oral and Written) A quick way to check for comprehension is by asking "What is this about?" during and/or after reading. An oral retelling can be done "on the run" and gives a good idea of whether or not kids are applying strategies to help them understand. To collect samples, periodically tape-record

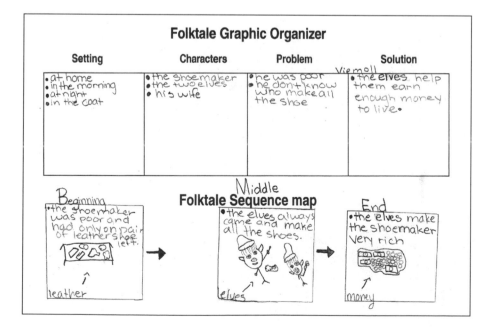

figure 1.3 *Viemoll retells* The Elves and the Shoemaker *with a flow map.*

figure 1.4 A written retelling of "The Shady Tree" provides information about how the student synthesizes.

Viemell

A long time ago in China, there lived a rich man. In his front house there grew a big cypress tree in his garden. One day, there was a man walking pass the richman's garden. He was sweting, hot and tired. The rich man notices that he was going to rest under his because he was sweting, hot and tired. The man did rest under the rich man tree. When the rich man saw him sitting under the tree. So he ran out of the house and ordered him to leave. The villiger said why he needed to leave. The rich man said that the road is puplic property. It's paid for by the tax payers. The villiger told the rich man that if the villigers could sell the tres, the rich man agreed him the two of them talk about the price amount. The man paid the rich man the money. But the man insisted the rich man gave him a deed for the shade. After they paid the money, the man came everyday to sit under the shade and sometimes he even bring his friend with him. He could even rest in the rich man bedroom. The richman wanted to get rid of the villiger. The richman gave a big party. People arrived with their fancy cloth on. But the man was not dressed in their find cloths. When the people sawed them they lauged and laughed.

students retelling text. Written retellings also serve as a record of growth over time. Samples can be assessed with a scoring guide for evaluating retelling. Story maps and flow maps are another way for students to retell text. For students at the beginning levels of English, drawing their retellings in one of these forms makes it possible for them to communicate their understanding of the text. Samples of retellings in different formats can be added to a literacy portfolio as evidence of growth over time.

Student Think-Alouds Asking students to think aloud about the strategies they are using as they read through a text gives information about how they orchestrate strategy use. This gives an indication of their abilities to internalize, use, and explain their thinking about their reading. Interviewing students about their thinking process indicates what strategies they are using as well as which strategies need to be taught. Notes taken as students think aloud while they read can be added to a literacy portfolios to demonstrate growth over time.

Teacher Observations During Reading Taking anecdotal records as students read independently and with partners provides evidence of how they use strategies as they read. Keeping a chart with students' names, dates of observations, and anecdotal notes demonstrates growth over time for how students apply strategies during independent reading and other reading activities. This gives information about how students are gradually taking on the responsibility for their own strategy use.

"Major Point Interview for Readers" (Keene and Zimmerman, Mosaic of Thought, *1997)* This is a set of rubrics to evaluate how students are using strategies, as well as how they think aloud while they read and how they retell text. These can be used all at the same time or individually to determine what students know and are able to do with strategies in their reading, and then to plan appropriate instruction. They can also be used as a beginning and a final assessment to determine students' growth over time and the effect of instruction.

Strategy Application Notebooks A simple way to collect and document students' use of strategies is to use strategy application notebooks. This involves inexpensive spiral notebooks, lots of sticky notes, two- and three- column charts, and other ways to organize strategy use. As students complete small-group strategy lessons, they use the strategy application notebook for their responses. It serves as a portfolio of sorts for strategy use. It also functions as a scaffold for students because they can refer to previous strategy lessons for support.

figure 1.5 *Strategy application notebooks hold students' work with strategies.*

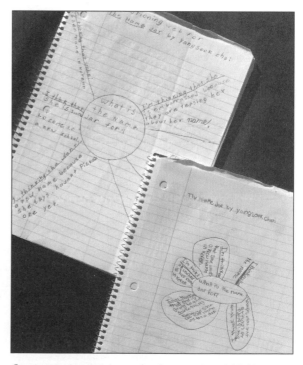

figure 1.6 *Questioning webs show students' thinking about their questions.*

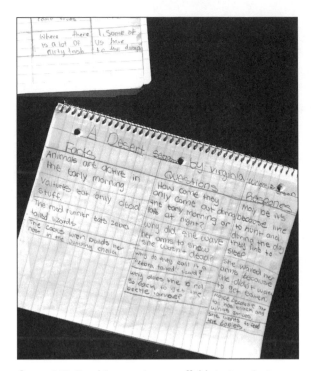

figure 1.7 *Graphic organizers scaffold strategy instruction for students.*

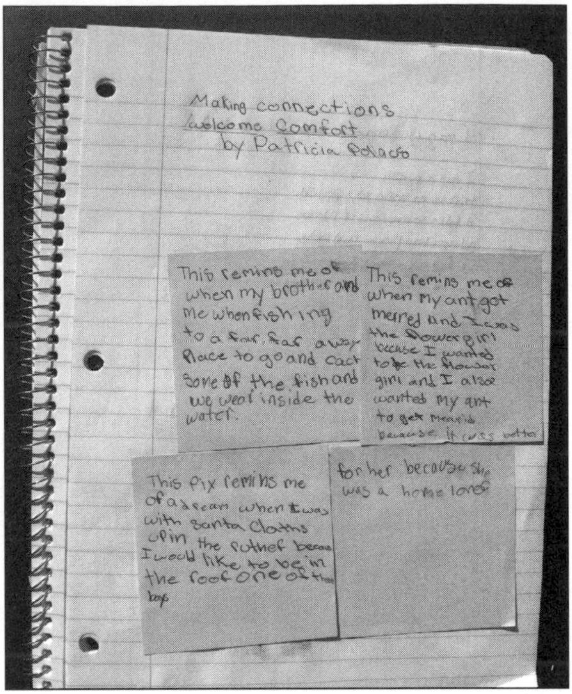

figure 1.8 *Sticky notes hold students' connections in strategy application notebooks.*

What Outey says about assessing students' use of strategies and comprehension of text:

> Initially, I like to talk to kids about their reading. By talking to them I can tell where they are. I use it as a base to plan my instruction. After that I use more formal assessments like the rubrics for the strategies. I also check to see how the students are doing on their end-of-unit reading assessments to make sure that what they are learning about using strategies to understand their reading transfers to the reading comprehension assessments.

How do you know your kids are getting it? And what do you do if they don't get it? It all starts with assessing students. How can you plan appropriate instruction if you don't know where kids are, especially since reading is an in-the-head behavior? There's also the process of ongoing evaluation, which is important to providing effective instruction. But what does this look like with reading comprehension strategies?

Step 1: To begin, determine priorities and decide whether to assess students' use of all strategies at the beginning or to assess only the strategy that will be studied. Depending on who the students are and where they are now, look at the assessments and determine what they need to learn and when they will need it. Use a variety of assessments to evaluate how students think aloud, use schema (make connections), infer, ask questions, determine what is important in text, monitor comprehension, visualize and create mental images, synthesize, and retell text. Also, it often makes sense to incorporate an assessment of strategy use with a running record of text reading.

Step 2: The next step is to set goals. They need to be high, worthwhile, and standards based, but still appropriate for these students at this time in this instructional environment. For example, for older students at the beginning levels of English, assessment may show little if any use of strategies. Lessons incorporating beginning strategy use can then be developed for these students, using wordless picture books and techniques such as picture walks (see Chapter 2, page 31) to provide comprehensible input, with the goal of introducing a strategy and using it on text with high levels of picture support.

Step 3: Now comes the instruction. It's planned to help students attain the goals that were set based on the initial assessments. The lessons need to provide comprehensible input and ways for students to connect the new learning to prior knowledge, information about the strategy, guided active involvement using the strategy, and opportunities to practice in other contexts.

Step 4: Next up? Evaluate student learning in light of the goals and the instruction. Look back at the goals that were set based on the initial assessments and then evaluate how the instruction helped students meet the goals.

Step 5: It's important to provide timely, meaningful feedback to students about their level of accomplishment based on the assessments. Working with students to use a scoring guide or rubric to evaluate their work helps them understand where they are and what they need to do next to improve. Once they understand the rubric, they can also evaluate each other's work and provide feedback.

Step 6: This is the time for teacher reflection. Look back at the student learning. Did the instructional design help move the students along and provide support? What went well? What would you do differently next time?

Step 7: Based on the lesson evaluation, set new goals. Just as before, the goals need to be high, worthwhile, and standards based, but still appropriate for these students at this time in this instructional environment. In this way, the process of initial assessment, goal setting, teaching, evaluation, reflection, reassessment, and setting new goals continues. Using this pattern of frequent, ongoing assessment, students show growth in strategy use, and comprehension continues to improve.

Selecting Books for Small-Group Strategy Instruction

After an initial assessment of strategy use, the logical next step is selecting books to use with English Language Learners during small-group strategy instruction. Book selection is very important and should not be rushed. Sharon Taberski (2000) suggests:

> Knowing my books and my children, and making a match between them, is one of the most important things I do—and one of the most demanding. It is exacting work that has led me to adjust my priorities in how I use my planning and class time. . . . I think about the children I am teaching and their needs. I think about how the books in my classroom support and challenge readers. And I think about which books are most likely to make a difference in each child's reading life. (p. 137)

With English Language Learners, there are additional considerations for selecting books for strategy instruction.

Assess students' oral fluency in their primary language. Begin by talking with students in their primary language. If you do not speak the language, find someone who does, such as a community volunteer, a custodian, or another teacher. It is important to get an idea of the student's oral fluency in their primary language, because this gives an indication of the level of literacy they have in that language. Research clearly shows (Cummins 2000) how important a student's primary language is for their personal and educational development.

Find out about the students' family background and interests in reading. Interview their families about the students. Ask questions such as What does the student like to do? What does the family do on weekends? Does the family go to the library?

Develop a profile of each student. This profile might include the student's age, family background, culture and language, stage of language proficiency, interests, school experience, and other information.

Determine if the text is culturally relevant. Culturally relevant texts "connect to students' lives not just to their cultural heritage." A good reason for choosing books that are culturally relevant is that readers "can more easily construct meaning from a text that contains familiar elements because their background knowledge helps them make predictions and inferences about the story" (Freeman and Freeman 2004).

Evaluate the supportive nature of the text. Look at the layout of the text, the use of pictures and whether or not they support the text, the amount of text, the level of the vocabulary, and the prior knowledge necessary to understand the text. Will the text provide support for readers?

Choose books that allow for flexibility when modeling strategy use. Consider whether the book is appropriate for modeling the use of a strategy in isolation or whether it can be used to show how readers construct meaning by orchestrating the use of several strategies as they read.

Decide if the book is appropriate for the ages of the students and if it matches their interests. Including students' interests in book selection increases their motivation for reading.

Check on the availability of the text. We created our book lists from the multitude of wonderful books available to use to teach strategies. In each chapter we list a few great books, but there are many other possibilities. Some wonderful texts go out of print. Public and school libraries often provide good collections of older stories. Online used-book sellers are another way to find out-of-print selections.

How does Outey select books for English Language Learners?

I'm looking for books with easy text. Not just a few words on the page, but books that are easy for the children to understand. It's the same as with the *Los Angeles Times*. They make sure to keep a reading level that means most people will be able to access the content. I also look for books the children can relate to their own culture and experience. For older students, I especially look for books that will broaden their thinking—sometimes in a book they give you the answer and it's right there. Instead, I look for books that encourage them to think by making connections, asking questions, inferring, determining importance in text, and synthesizing.

Honestly, I also look for books that give value to parents. I want to find books that show a positive relationship between parents and their children. In a way, I'm a traditional person, and I value these traditional relationships.

Importance of Genre

It's also important to keep genres in mind when selecting texts. Realistic fiction, informational and nonfiction texts, poetry, and folktales and fables provide a wide variety from which to choose. To ensure that English Language Learners' linguistic and cultural backgrounds are represented in the curriculum, it is important to include folktales and fables. By selecting folktales and fables for strategy instruction, a variety of cultural values and perspectives are included, facilitating students' ability to connect their background experience and prior knowledge to what they are learning.

Outey thinks it is important for children to learn folktales and fables:

In our culture we teach values through folktales and fables. Here, you read to children before bed. In Cambodia, we tell folktales and fables to children, but it is the grandparents who do this in the evenings. This is important because it keeps family relationships together—grandchildren and grandparents. We see grandparents as "the living proof—the living book." So it is really important for grandparents to pass the folktales and fables on to their grandchildren because they have the life experience. Also, ours is an oral storytelling tradition, and our folktales and fables are not usually written down.

Because they contain values from the culture, it's very important for children to learn folktales and fables from different cultures. In this way they can see the similarities and differences among people and learn to live in a wider world.

Checklist for Book Selection

☐ Assess students' oral fluency in the primary language.

☐ Find out about each student's family background and interests in reading. Interview each family.

☐ Develop a profile of each student.

☐ Determine if the text is culturally relevant.

☐ Evaluate the supportive nature of the text.

☐ Choose books that allow for flexibility when modeling strategy use.

☐ Decide if the book is appropriate for the ages of the students and if it matches their interests.

☐ Check on the availability of the text.

PREPRODUCTION

2

Younger English Language Learners in Real Time

Lee and Nelson are on their way to work with their reading teacher, Outey. One meanders slowly along, observing the lunchtime activity. Although their lunch recess just ended, he seems lost in the fourth-grade basketball games on the playground. The other walks quickly, arriving ahead of his partner. Both first graders enter the classroom, locate their reading folders, and sit down at the kidney-shaped table. Outey greets them in Khmer, and both respond appropriately. They begin by reading familiar, easy texts in English and then start on a new book. As they page through the new text, she thinks aloud, "This book is about the farm and the animals who live there. It reminds me of when I taught kindergarten and we took a field trip to the farm."

As Outey continues through the book, pointing at the pictures to identify the animals and their different activities, she asks the boys, "What does the book remind you of? Did you go on a field trip to the farm when you were in kindergarten?"

"Pigs and cows," says Nelson as he points to the appropriate picture in the book.

"Yes," answers Lee.

figure 2.1 (above left) Outey works with Nelson and Lee.

figure 2.2 (above center) Field trips, like this one to the aquarium, help students learn concepts and language as they view the exhibits and make colorfully decorated fish.

figure 2.3 (above right) Songs such as "Old MacDonald" offer students a way to respond to text.

"What do the pictures remind you of? Point to the animals in the book that you saw on your field trip. Can you make a connection?" Outey asks.

But when another teacher joins their group, the students are no longer comfortable speaking and everything changes. These students become quiet and watchful. This is not unusual for students in the Preproduction stage. "Hi!" says Nelson, but Lee drops his eyes and hunches over his work, as if to say, "Don't bother me, I'm reading."

Can these first-grade beginning English Language Learners use strategies to understand their reading? By using books and realia that provide comprehensible input, choosing topics students can relate to their background experience, creating a low-anxiety environment, and encouraging students to respond physically as well as verbally, Outey helps her students use the strategies of making connections to text, questioning, visualizing, and inferring.

Lesson Plans for Younger English Language Learners

1: Making Connections

Teaching Moves

Start-up/Connection Start by saying something such as, "Let's take a look at the photographs from your field trip to the farm." Talk about the photos one at a time. Identify the students and the farm animals in the pictures. Pass around the photos for students to look at individually.

Give Information "The book we are reading today is called *Farm Animals*." Hold up the book so children can see it. "It is filled with photographs of animals from the farm. This book reminds me of our field trip to the farm. Look at the cover. There's a picture of a pig." Point to the picture of the pig on the cover. "Which photograph from the field trip to the farm does it remind you of?" Lay photographs in front of students to allow them to search for the photo of the pigs. "Yes! I agree with you. That's the picture that it reminds me of. I made a connection from the book about farm animals to one of the photographs of the field trip to the farm, and so did you."

Active Involvement "Let's look through the book and see if the pictures remind us of any other photographs from the field trip." Move slowly through the book, discussing the photo on each page, using language such as "making connections" and "it reminds me of." Allow time for the students to locate the photos from the field trip. Have them point to show their connections.

Off You Go "Now I am going to give you a copy of the book, and I want you to work with a partner to read it and make connections to the photos from the field trip. Share your connections with your partner." Have multiple copies of the book so that students can work with one or two others to make their own connections. Encourage students to interact with each other.

Instructional Materials

- Photographs of field trip to the farm
- *Farm Animals* (DK Lift-the-Flap) (board book with photos of farm animals)

2: Asking Questions

Teaching Moves

Start-up/Connection "We've been reading books about farm animals and making our own connections. We talked about how these books reminded us of the trip to the farm. Let's take a look at one of the books again to remind us about our connections." As a group, quickly go through the book *Farm Animals* to talk about the connections from the previous readings. Have students indicate, verbally or by pointing, which pages in the book reminded them of the field trip to the farm.

Give Information "Today we have a new book to read. The book is *Who Says Quack?* by Jerry Smith. This book also has photos of farm animals just like *Farm Animals* and *A Day at Greenhill Farm*. It also asks questions. When we ask questions as we read, it helps us understand the story. Let's go through the book together and see if we can answer the questions it asks." As you start the book, think aloud to demonstrate how to answer the question "Who says quack?" For example, "I think it must be the duck who says, 'Quack,' because I saw that on TV," or "I heard the ducks quacking at the farm."

Active Involvement Consider giving each student a copy of the book so they can be actively engaged with the text. After demonstrating how to answer the question on the cover, continue answering the questions as you read through the book with the students. Use pointing and gesturing to convey meaning. Encourage students to point and gesture at the pictures and the text to make themselves understood.

Off You Go After reading through the story and answering the questions, give students a variety of books about farm animals and have them think about their own questions. Watch to see how they manage the task. Do they ask yes or no questions? Do they model from the story and ask questions like, "Who says quack?" Or do they just sit quietly, since students are often still at the listening stage? This is just a first step in asking questions. The more you know about your students and whether or not they ask questions about their reading, the better you will be able to plan instruction to encourage them to ask questions.

3: Visualizing—Creating Mental Images

Teaching Moves

Start-up/Connection "We've been reading some books about the farm and farm animals." (Hold up the books for the students while reading the titles.) "We've read *Farm Animals*, *A Day at Greenhill Farm*, *Who Says Quack?*, and *Big Red Barn*. We've made connections to our stories and we have asked questions." Although this is the silent period, students can use some time to look over the books they have already read, think about the texts, and process what is being said.

Give Information "Today we will read a story called *Rosie's Walk*, by Pat Hutchins. While we read the story, we're going to visualize what is happening. We are going to act out what happens to Rosie and the fox who is chasing her. We want to make a movie in our minds about what is happening in the story. We want to see it just as if we were at the movies."

Active Involvement "Let's read the story together first and see what happens to Rosie and the fox." Read each page of the book and stop to let the students see what Rosie is doing and what happens to the fox in each of the different scenarios. Encourage the students to talk about the pictures or to point to the various problems the fox is having.

Off You Go "Now we are going to have different students pretend to act out the story. Who would like to be Rosie? And who would like to be the fox?" Choose a volunteer for each character. If there are more than two volunteers, students can act out the story more than once. It's very short. "Rosie is going to begin and the fox is going to follow her. She starts out on a walk and goes 'across the yard.' Before we begin, let's decide where the yard should be." Use the picture from the book to make it clear to the students what a yard is and then have them choose a location in the classroom or on the playground to be the yard. Continue by choosing a location for the pond, the haystack, the mill, the fence, the beehives, and the chicken coop, using the pictures in the book for comprehensible input. Once the locations are chosen, read the story slowly as the volunteers act it out.

4: Inferring and Predicting

Teaching Moves

Start-up/Connection "We're going to start today by singing a song we know. The song is called 'Old MacDonald Had a Farm.' Here we go!" As you sing along with the children, include photos or pictures of the animals to provide comprehensible input and help them understand the lyrics. Stop singing as each animal is introduced and hold up a picture of the animal. Say the name of the animal for the students and point to the picture as you do so to help them understand what you are saying. Then continue singing. Use the recorded version of the song from the *Wee Sing* tape, or other recordings, if it helps to support the students as they sing.

Give Information "We are reading a book called *Old MacDonald Had a Farm*. What does this remind you of? Yes! This is the same story as the song we were just singing. Let's read through the book and see if we can use the pictures to predict what animals will be on Old MacDonald's farm."

Active Involvement: Read each page. As you come to the cutout that shows a part of the animal, say, "Let's predict! What animal is this?" After the students predict what animal they think it will be, turn the page and let them confirm their prediction. Continue predicting and/or inferring until the end of the book. (See figure 2.4.)

Instructional Materials

- *Old MacDonald Had a Farm* illus. by Carol Jones
- "Old MacDonald Had a Farm" from *Wee Sing, 25th Anniversary Celebration* by Pamela Bealle and Susan Nipp

Off You Go "We are learning how to predict when we read, so let's make a prediction chart to put up on the wall. Look at this large piece of chart paper. It's titled 'Let's predict! What animal is this?' Everyone is going to get a white circle [three inches in diameter]. On the white circle draw part of an animal. Be careful. Your drawing should help someone predict which animal it is. For example, you might draw a pigtail if you want people to predict that your animal is a pig. Then on the back of the white circle in large black letters write the name of the animal." Demonstrate for the students as you explain what you want them to do. Students can work together to decide which parts of the animal to draw and then help each other with spelling the names of the animals. Then say, "After you finish drawing and writing the name on the back, take a piece of tape and tape the top of the circle to the prediction chart. Make sure the name of the animal is hiding on the back and that people can see part of your animal on the front of the circle. We'll use this chart to practice making predictions." Demonstrate as you talk. Hang the finished chart on the wall to use for predicting.

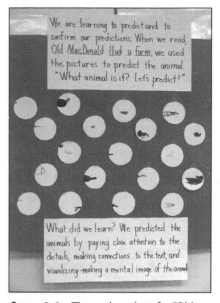

figure 2.4   *The anchor chart for "Old MacDonald" shows how beginning English Language Learners predict as they read.*

Books for Teaching Strategies to Younger English Language Learners

Preproduction Level

Making Connections

Buzz by Janet Wong
Farm Animals (DK Lift-the-Flap)
Hats, Hats, Hats by Ann Morris
In My Family, En mi familia by Carmen Lomas Garza
One Small Girl by Jennifer Chan

Asking Questions

Brown Bear, Brown Bear, What Do You See? by Bill Martin and Eric Carle
Have You Seen My Duckling? by Nancy Tafuri
Is It Red? Is It Yellow? Is It Blue? by Tana Hoban
Where's Spot? Lift the Flap Series by Eric Hill
Who Says Quack? by Jerry Smith

Visualizing

"Barnyard Dance" from *Rhinoceros TAP* by Sandra Boynton
Pancakes for Breakfast by Tomie dePaola
Puppy Trouble (pop-up version) by Alexandra Day
Rosie's Walk (big book version) by Pat Hutchins

I Spy Treasure Hunt: A Book of Picture Riddles (I Spy books) by
Walter Wick

Inferring

Round Is a Mooncake: A Book of Shapes by Roseanne Thong
Red Is a Dragon: A Book of Colors by Roseanne Thong
Old MacDonald Had a Farm illus. by Carol Jones
My Friend Rabbit by Eric Rohmann
Zoom by Istvan Banyai

Older English Language Learners in Real Time

Every fall as the middle school where Juli taught settled in to a new school year, teachers discovered students in their classes who didn't speak any English. Most often the students were recently arrived from Mexico or Cambodia. They came on the bus or in car pools wearing new school uniforms and carrying backpacks filled with school supplies. This school wasn't a neighborhood school. Kids rode clear across town to experience wide open grassy fields without locked gates. Canals flowed to the ocean on two sides of the school, making a home for snowy egrets and seagulls. In the spring mallard ducks walked their ducklings from the apartment complex across the street, through the school walkways, across the grass field, and into the canals. The university was down the street, and a historic rancho was just up the hill. But the idyllic setting didn't change the fact that these kids didn't speak English.

For these older English Language Learners—sixth-, seventh-, and eighth-graders—the demands of learning a new language were complicated by grade-level academic content. They needed to learn math, science, and history at the same time they were learning to read and write in English. To meet students' needs, beginning English speakers were grouped together at each grade level. This allowed teachers to provide comprehensible input to build the background they needed for pre-algebra, electrical circuits, and learning about the ancient worlds of Egypt, Greece, and Rome.

To a great extent students were successful if they mastered creating mental images and learned to visualize through pictures, realia, and hands-on projects and tasks. The importance of visually supporting learning for beginning English Language Learners came through loud and clear as Juli developed a collection of wonderful wordless picture books. Kids loved the David Weisner books (*Free Fall*, *Tuesday*, and *Sector 7*). They wondered at *The Mysteries of Harris Burdick* by Chris Van Allsburg and *Time Flies* by Eric Rohmann. Using wordless books, beginning English speakers were able to use strategies to think and process information at high levels.

Teachers thought students had "adjusted" if they learned and made progress. But students had different ideas. After several months at school, one sixth-grade girl wrote (translated from Spanish), "I have lived here for a year and months. I do not like living in the United States because I like Mexico more."

"It was very different in my country," another girl wrote in Spanish. Not bad, just different.

One thing that helped these students ultimately make the transition to school in the United States was small-group strategy instruction. Juli used reading and writing workshop to set up her classroom for beginning English Language Learners. By using a workshop setting for literacy instruction and allowing students to work in small groups of as many as five, they slowly began to feel more comfortable with each other and with English. Through instructional conversations they took on the use of reading comprehension strategies while they learned English. The small-group instruction acted as a scaffold for their learning and allowed for a gradual release of responsibility (Pearson and Gallagher 1983). As time passed, students took on more and more of the responsibility for monitoring their use of strategies and clarifying unknown vocabulary and concepts as they read.

Lesson Plans for Older English Language Learners

1: Making Connections

Teaching Moves

Start-up/Connection   One of the techniques we use for older students at this level is to mask the text in a book so students focus on the pictures. We call it text masking. Sometimes we cover the text with paper or sticky notes, and sometimes we just focus on the pictures. This technique is particularly effective with books that have illustrations that evoke strong responses. Here's what we tell the kids: "This book has beautiful pictures of people working in the fields. We covered up the words so that we'll just think about the pictures. Let's take a picture walk through the book together, focusing on and discussing just the pictures." Go through the book page by page, looking carefully at the illustrations and commenting on them. Remember to speak slowly and emphasize key words. As you talk, point and gesture toward the pictures to help students understand.

What is a picture walk? A picture walk is when a student looks at the pictures before reading the book to get an idea of what the story is about. It sets the stage for reading and approximates how readers naturally approach text: they browse through the book first. Teachers should teach students how to take a picture walk through a book during shared reading sessions. The teacher and children talk their way through the pictures, anticipating what might be happening in the story.

Give Information   "The book we are reading today is called *Gathering the Sun*." Many students who come from agricultural backgrounds will have connections to the pictures of people working in the fields. "I'm going to look through the pictures in the book and stop when I come to a place that reminds me of something." As you slowly look through the pictures in the book, emphasize the key vocabulary and make simple connections to the text.

Instructional Materials

- *Gathering the Sun: An Alphabet in English and Spanish* by Alma Flor Ada (wonderful pictures that evoke the life of an agricultural worker, with simple poems in Spanish and English)
- **Strategy application notebooks**
- **Markers**

Active Involvement As you read through the book, allow plenty of time for students to look at the pictures, listen to you make connections to the pictures, and think about their connections to different pictures. Students are in the silent period, so provide opportunities for them to use gestures, pointing, and so on to communicate.

Off You Go "Now that we've read all the way through the book, I'm going to give you strategy application notebooks and markers. I want you to draw something that the book reminds you of." Model how to do this by drawing one of your connections for the students and thinking aloud as you draw. Then give students the opportunity to draw their connections, as in figures 2.5 and 2.6.

2: Asking Questions

Teaching Moves

Start-up/Connection "The book I am going to read aloud has pictures that tell a story, but there are also lots of questions we can ask about the story and the pictures. Let's take a picture walk through the book together." Go through the book page by page, looking carefully at the illustrations and commenting on them. Remember to speak slowly and emphasize key words. As you talk, point and gesture toward the pictures to help students understand.

Instructional Materials

■ *How Many Days to America?* by Eve Bunting

■ Overhead transparency for anchor chart labeled "Questions: Before, During, and After Reading"

■ Strategy application notebooks

figure 2.5 *Art provides a medium for making connections for students in the silent period.*

figure 2.6 *Students make connections with the text through drawing.*

Give Information "The book we are reading today is called *How Many Days to America?*" Many students who come from other countries will have background experiences about coming to America in different ways. "Before I read through the book, I'm going to write some of my questions on the overhead." (Example: Do the people in the story want to come to America?) "Now I'm going to read through the book and stop when I come to a place where I have a question." Continue to model by asking your questions aloud and list them on the overhead transparency. As you slowly read through the book, emphasize the key vocabulary and think aloud about yes and no questions about the text. After reading, write one or two questions on the chart.

Active Involvement Consider giving each student a copy of the book so they can be actively engaged with the text. As you read through the book, allow plenty of time for students to look at the pictures, listen to you read aloud, and listen to your questions about the text and pictures. Students should speak only if they volunteer. You are modeling how to ask questions as you read, not calling on students to answer them. Continue to list your questions about the story on an anchor chart on an overhead transparency. At this level, the emphasis should be on the pictures and developing an understanding of the story, not on having students generate their own questions.

Anchor Chart/Overhead

Questions Before, During, and After Reading
How Many Days to America? by Eve Bunting

Before Reading

Do they have money to pay for the boat?
Do the people in the story want to come to America?
Are the people in the story afraid?

During Reading

Did the father take his wife's wedding ring and necklace to pay for
  the trip?
Was the whale friendly?
On the last page, is the family scared?

After Reading

Do the people in the family have jobs?
Is there a place for them to live?
Will they have food?

Off You Go "Now that we've read all the way through the book, I'm going to give you your strategy application notebooks. I want you to copy the chart/overhead for 'Questioning: Before, During, and After Reading' into your notebook. This will give you an example that you can use to help you remember to ask questions when you are reading." Students will be able to refer to this chart and use it as a model for asking questions about other books. In this way, the lesson starts off with the teacher's questions and graduates to the students coming up with their own questions.

3: Visualizing—Creating Mental Images

Teaching Moves

Instructional Materials

- Books by David Weisner (*Tuesday, Sector 7,* and *June 29, 1999*)
- Strategy application notebooks

Start-up/Connection   "Today we are going to read a book by David Weisner. He tells his stories with many pictures and illustrations and just a few words. First, let's take a look at his book *Tuesday.*" As you take a picture walk through the book, provide time for thinking and for talking about the pictures, if students feel comfortable speaking.

Give Information   "When we read, we make pictures, or movies, in our minds to help us understand what we are reading. Take a minute and think about the story and how the pictures helped you understand. Let's look through the pictures again as you think about how they help you understand the author's story."

Active Involvement   Have students work in pairs to draw their visualizations from *Tuesday* in their strategy application notebooks. Ask them what they think will happen after the end of the book, or what happened between two of the pictures from the story. This technique is called filling in the gaps. Students draw a visualization of what they think happened after one picture and before the next, as in figures 2.7 and 2.8.

figure 2.7   *This is a student's mental image of "If pigs could fly..." from* Tuesday *by David Weisner.*

figure 2.8   *A beginning English Language Learner visualizes in a strategy application notebook.*

Off You Go Have additional copies of the books *Sector 7* and *June 29, 1999* for the students in the group. When time allows, have students take a picture walk through the books, working either with a partner or independently to visualize the story. If they choose to draw visualizations of the books, they can use their strategy application notebooks for their drawings.

4: Inferring

Teaching Moves

Instructional Materials
■ *Time Flies* **by Eric Rohmann**

Start-up/Connection "Today we are going to read a book by Eric Rohmann. It's titled *Time Flies*. This book gives us lots of opportunities to predict and infer. First, let's take a look at the cover of his book." Provide time for thinking and listening as you talk about the cover of the book. Point and gesture to provide comprehensible input.

Give Information "When we read, we make predictions. We think about what might happen next. Then as we read more, we confirm or contradict our predictions. This helps us understand what we are reading. Let's go through the pictures and predict what we think will happen next in the book." Although students are at the preproduction level and have little expressive English, using academic vocabulary (words such as *predictions, confirm, contradict, predict*) serves as an introduction to these words and concepts. It is especially important that teachers make the lesson comprehensible and identify when they are predicting, as well as when they are confirming or contradicting their predictions. For example, a teacher gives a clue such as, "Now I'm predicting, I'm looking at the picture and I'm thinking. . . ."

Active Involvement As you go through the pictures in the book, model how you predict what will happen next. Have students indicate with thumbs-up or thumbs-down whether or not they agree with your prediction. Then turn the page and confirm or contradict your prediction.

Off You Go Have additional copies of the book *Free Fall* by David Weisner for the students in the group. When time allows, have students take a picture walk through the book, working either with a partner or independently. Provide opportunities for them to work with a partner and go through the book predicting what will happen next and using a thumbs-up or thumbs-down to show whether or not they agree with each other. If students are not comfortable speaking, provide opportunities for them to look through the Weisner book. This allows them to rehearse how to predict "in their heads."

Books for Teaching Strategies to Older English Language Learners

Preproduction Level

Making Connections

Bread, Bread, Bread by Ann Morris

Family Pictures, Cuadros de familia by Carmen Lomas Garza
Gathering the Sun: An Alphabet in English and Spanish by Alma
  Flor Ada
On the Go by Ann Morris
Shoes, Shoes, Shoes by Ann Morris

Asking Questions

An Ocean World by Peter Sis
Diving Dolphins, DK Readers by Karen Wallace
Four Hungry Kittens by Emily Arnold McCully
How Many Days to America? by Eve Bunting
Rockets and Spaceships, DK Readers by Karen Wallace

Visualizing—Making Mental Images

Can You See What I See? (I Spy books) *by* William Wick
Home by Jeannie Baker
June 29, 1999 by David Weisner
Sector 7 by David Weisner
Snow Music by Lynn Rae Perkins
Tuesday by David Weisner

Inferring

A Day, A Dog by Gabrielle Vincent
Don't Let the Pigeon Ride the Bus! by Mo Willems
Free Fall by David Weisner
The Mysteries of Harris Burdick by Chris Van Allsburg
Time Flies by Eric Rohmann

Wordless Picture Books

Use discretion when choosing wordless picture books for younger students. Many contain sophisticated content and themes appropriate for older students. Just because it's a picture book, don't assume that it is intended for young children.

Abstract Alphabet by Paul Cox
Anno's Counting Book by Mitsumasa Anno
Clementina's Cactus by Ezra Jack Keats
Clown by Quentin Blake
A Day, A Dog by Gabrielle Vincent
Dinosaur! by Peter Sis
Follow Carl! by Alexandra Day
Four Hungry Kittens by Emily Arnold McCully
Free Fall by David Wiesner
Good Dog, Carl! and other Carl stories, by Alexandra Day

The Grey Lady and the Strawberry Snatcher by Molly Bang
Home by Jeannie Baker
June 29, 1999 by David Weisner
Magpie Magic: A Tale of Colorful Mischief by April Wilson
The Mysteries of Harris Burdick by Chris Van Allsburg
An Ocean World by Peter Sis
Oh! by Josse Goffin
Pancakes for Breakfast by Tomie dePaola
Peep! by Kevin Luthardt
Re-Zoom by Istvan Banyai
The Ring by Lisa Maizlish
Sector 7 by David Wiesner
Sidewalk Circus by Paul Fleischman and Kevin Hawkes
The Snowman by Raymond Briggs
Time Flies by Eric Rohmann
Tuesday by David Wiesner
You Can't Take a Balloon into the National Gallery by
 Jacqueline Weitzman
Why? by Nikolai Popov
Zoom by Istvan Banyai

EARLY PRODUCTION

3

Younger English Language Learners in Real Time

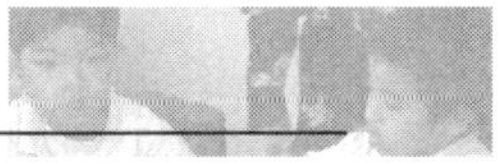

The first graders parade into the classroom as Outey organizes the plastic fruit and easy concept books on her table. Her goal is to teach these Cambodian students about opposites in English. She starts by previewing the concept of opposites in Khmer, which is spoken in Cambodia. She wants English Language Learners to make connections between what they already know in Khmer and what they are learning about opposites in English.

The Preview-Review strategy allows Outey to check with students before the lesson starts to make sure they understand the concept of opposites in Khmer. Then at the end of the lesson, she'll review what they have learned about opposites in English, using their primary language. Primary language support is an important strategy to help beginning English Language Learners acquire English. It allows the teacher to provide background information before the lesson in English and review for understanding at the end of the lesson.

It's very quiet as Outey starts, and then suddenly everyone is answering in Khmer. Listening to their reaction to the preview of the lesson, it's easy to tell that the children have lots of prior knowledge about opposites. After the preview, Outey turns to English and reads aloud several simple books about

figure 3.1 *(above left) Students work together to plan their predictions.*

figure 3.2 *(above center) Students draw pictures to learn how to predict what will come next.*

figure 3.3 *(above right) Visiting the aquarium for a celebration of Asian Pacific cultures allows for hands-on learning activities such as cutting paper lanterns.*

39

opposites. Students begin to chime in with English as they catch on to the predictable pattern of the books. Then she hands out a pile of plastic fruit to each child in the small group. She uses these realia to have students practice opposites such as up/down, over/under, and big/little. Students chatter away in English as they do these hands-on, comprehensible activities.

Next, it's time to work with a partner and do some writing. Outey hands out paper and pencils, and together they begin a list of opposites. She uses the large white board to model the task and then encourages each set of partners to complete a list of opposites by working from the easy books she has provided. Talking back and forth in English, everyone successfully completes a list of at least five opposites.

After the lesson, Outey quickly uses Khmer to review with the students what they have learned. She finds they have mastered the simple opposites she presented and are ready to move on to the next level. The review helps her confirm that students are ready for more. She'll use this information to plan tomorrow's lesson.

Lesson Plans for Younger English Language Learners

1: Making Connections

Teaching Moves

Start-up/Connection Begin by using realia to give comprehensible input about the book *Mice and Beans*. Use small stuffed mice or pictures of mice and mousetraps. In addition, try making the recipe for rice and beans on the back cover of the book to provide background knowledge. It's a good idea to review the days of the week as well, since they are used to sequence the story. To encourage students to draw on their prior knowledge and make connections to the text, go through the book as a group, talking about each of the pictures and relating the realia and the recipe to the story.

Give Information As you read aloud *Mice and Beans* to students, model making text-to-self connections. Explain the strategy and demonstrate how it applies to the text by thinking aloud, "When I was reading this part, it reminded me of...." Quickly write your connections on a sticky note and post them on an anchor chart.

Active Involvement After the first read-aloud of the book, go through the book again. Encourage students to say the predictable parts of the text, the parts that repeat, along with you. This time have students share their connections as you read. Encourage them to act out their connections by role playing. As they tell their connections, write each connection on a sticky note. Give the sticky note to the student to post on the anchor chart, as in figure 3.4.

Instructional Materials

- Realia (such as small stuffed mice, pictures of mice, and mousetraps)
- *Mice and Beans* by Pam Munoz Ryan
- Anchor chart
- Strategy application notebook
- Collection of predictable texts at http://www.monroe.lib.in.us/childrens/predict.html Monroe County Public Library, Monroe County, Indiana

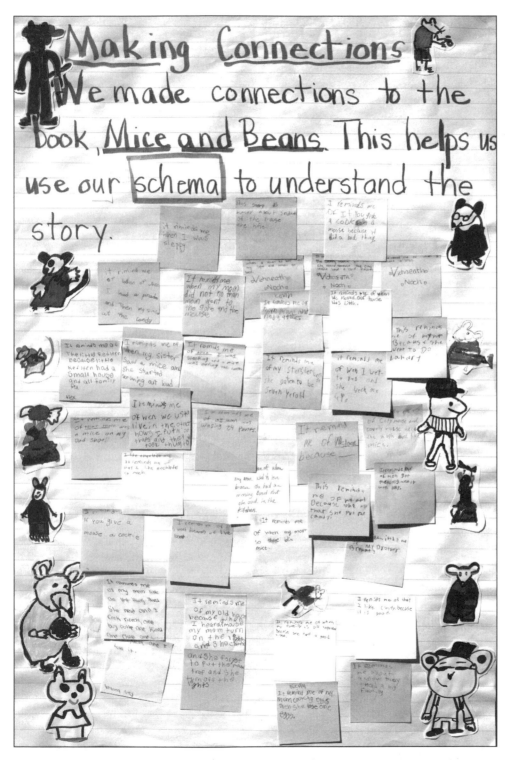

figure 3.4   *Anchor charts can be used to hold students' thinking about strategies.*

Off You Go Provide a collection of predictable books with which the students are familiar. Explain that they will be choosing books to read and reading with a partner. As they read, have them tell their connections to a partner. Then have them write their connections to the story on a sticky note and place it on a page in their strategy application notebook. Tell students that this is just like what they did when they put their connections on the anchor chart. (It is a good idea to model how to use the strategy application notebook before having students work on their own.)

2: Asking Questions

Teaching Moves

Start-up/Connection Begin by using realia to give comprehensible input about the book *The Wednesday Surprise*. Help students understand the relationship between the word *surprise* and birthday celebrations. To prepare students to ask questions about the text, go through the text as a group, talking about each picture and relating the realia to the story. For example, show the picture on pages 4 and 5 and talk about how the grandmother is sitting on the bench waiting for the bus. Point out the bus stop sign and other things going on in the picture.

Give Information "Before reading the book," writes Debbie Miller in *Reading with Meaning*, "I explain to the children that thoughtful readers ask questions not only as they read, but also before and after reading." As you read aloud *The Wednesday Surprise* to students, model asking questions before, during, and after reading. Explain that asking questions as you read helps you understand the story. Model by thinking aloud: "Before I read the story, this is a question I have." Write your questions on sticky notes and post them on an anchor chart.

Active Involvement After the first read-aloud of the book, go through the book again. This time have students share their questions as you read. Encourage them to share their questions with the group and then write them on a sticky note. Have students post the sticky notes on the anchor chart and organize them by before, during, and after reading the story. See figure 3.5.

Off You Go Provide a collection of books by Eve Bunting with which the students are familiar. Explain that they will work with a partner and choose books to read. As they read together, have them write their questions about the story on sticky notes and place them on a page in their strategy application notebooks. Tell students that this is just like what they did when they put their questions on the anchor chart. (It is a good idea to model how to use the strategy application notebook before having students work on their own.)

Instructional Materials

- **Realia** (pictures of grandparents and grandchildren doing things together, pictures of birthday celebrations)
- *The Wednesday Surprise* by Eve Bunting
- **Anchor chart labeled "Questions Before, During, and After Reading"**
- **Strategy application notebooks**
- **Other books by Eve Bunting**

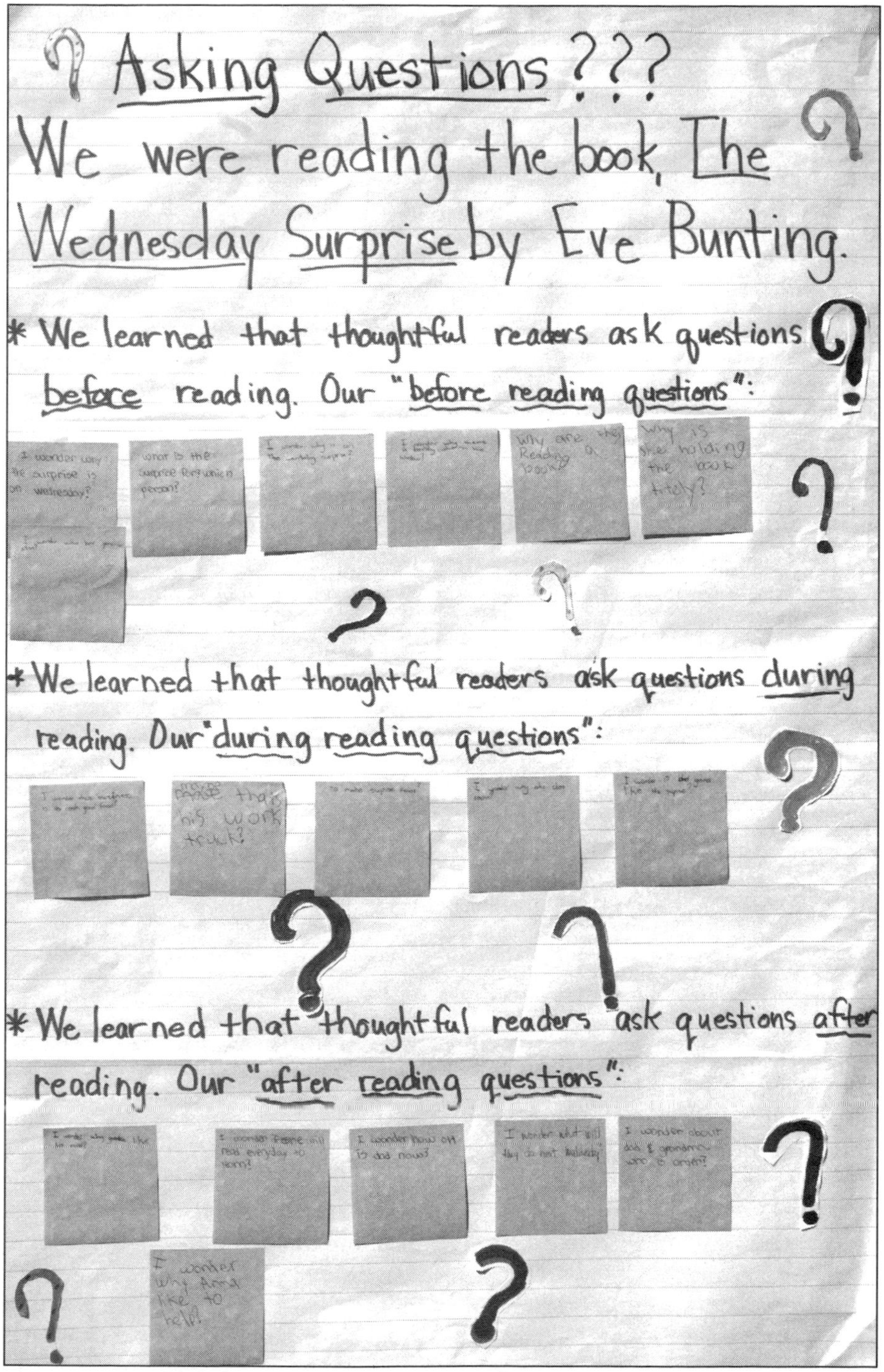

figure 3.5 *Students place their questions on sticky notes for an anchor chart about asking questions.*

Instructional Materials

■ Field trip opportu-
nity (for example,
aquarium, farm, zoo,
post office, fire sta-
tion, grocery store,
children's museum,
library)
■ Copies of the follow-
ing poems from *all
the small poems and
fourteen more* by
Valerie Worth:
"aquarium," "sea
lions," "seashell,"
"starfish," "octopus"
■ Drawings of students'
mental images (visual-
izations) of the poems

3: Visualizing—Creating Mental Images

Teaching Moves

Start-up/Connection Provide a field trip opportunity for students. (We went to the aquarium.) This promotes language acquisition and encourages the use of oral language. After the field trip, spend time with students talking about the experience. This helps them build background. Provide plenty of "think time" for students as you discuss the field trip. Encourage open dialog between the students.

Give Information Explain to students that making mental images and visualizing movies in your mind while you read helps readers understand. Tell them that they will be reading poems about some of the things they saw on the field trip. Hand out copies of several poems and do a shared reading with the group.

Active Involvement Have students draw their own visualizations of the poems in their strategy application notebooks. They can copy the short poem they choose in their notebook and then draw the visualization. Model by thinking aloud as you do your own drawing for one of the poems.

Off You Go After students draw their visualizations, have them exchange drawings with a partner. Have them compare the two visualizations. Encourage students to talk about the similarities and differences and what they think it means that we all see things differently. Encourage them to talk about how visualizing helps them understand the poems they are reading.

Instructional Materials

■ "Story Number Three,
The Artist" from
*George and Martha
Round and Round* by
James Marshall
■ Additional books
about George and
Martha by James
Marshall *(George and
Martha Back in Town,
George and Martha
Encore, George and
Martha Tons of Fun,
George and Martha:
The Complete Stories
of Two Best Friends)*
■ Anchor chart labeled
"What can you do to
help yourself infer the
meaning of a word?"

4: Inferring

Teaching Moves

Start-up/Connection This lesson focuses on using "Story Number Three, The Artist" from the book *George and Martha Round and Round,* but the lesson is easily adapted to any of the other stories in the George and Martha books. To build background for the story, explain that George and Martha are friends. Discuss how friends sometimes disagree. Also talk to children about what they know about artists. Explain that many artists paint and draw. Find out if the students like to paint or draw or have family members who do. Then take a picture walk through the story, discussing with the students what is happening in the pictures.

Give Information To teach students about inferring at the word stage, model how you wonder about the meanings of words as you read aloud the short story. Use the context from the pictures to infer the meanings. For example: "As I'm reading the first page, I'm wondering what the word *interference* means. So I check the picture and I notice that Martha is standing right behind George while he is painting. I bet he doesn't like that. Look at the expression on his face. He doesn't like it. I'm inferring that *interference* might mean that Martha is getting in the way." Be sure to use gestures and point to the places in the picture that helped you infer. Allow talking time. Students can talk to a partner about what they notice and what they infer. Make a chart with three columns labeled

"Word," "We infer it means," and "What helped us" (Miller 2002). Write the word *interference* in the first column. Fill in the other two columns as a model for the students, as in figure 3.6.

Active Involvement Read another story from the book *George and Martha Round and Round*. As you read each page, stop and let students infer the meaning of words that are unknown to them. Have students add the words and their inferences and what helped them infer to the chart.

Off You Go Provide other opportunities for students to read more George and Martha stories. Encourage them to work with a partner, to talk about how they infer the meanings of the unknown words, and to add the words to the anchor chart and fill in the columns.

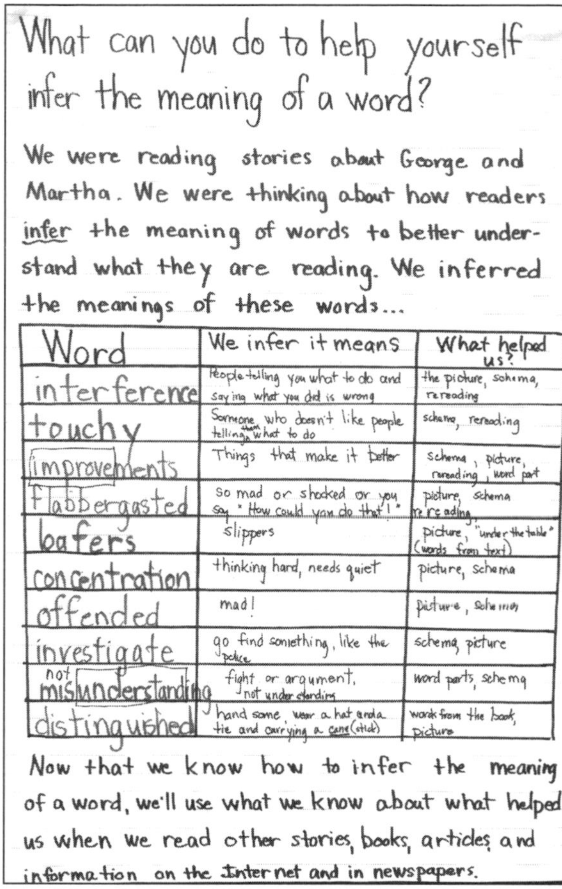

Books for Teaching Strategies to Younger English Language Learners

Early Production Stage

Making Connections

A Birthday Basket for Tia by Pat Mora
Families by Ann Morris
Mice and Beans by Pam Munoz Ryan
The Ugly Vegetables by Grace Lin
Yoko's Paper Cranes by Rosemary Wells

Asking Questions

Bedtime in the Southwest by Mona Hodgson
How Do Dinosaurs Get Well Soon? by Jane Yolen
Hush! by Minfong Ho
Peek! A Thai Hide-and-Seek by Minfong Ho
The Wednesday Surprise by Eve Bunting
Which Witch Is Which? by Judi Barrett

Visualizing

all the small poems and fourteen more by Valerie Worth
Creatures of the Earth, Sea, and Sky: Poems by Georgia Heard
Joseph Had a Little Overcoat by Simms Taback
The Wheels on the Bus by Paul Zelinsky
There Was an Old Lady Who Swallowed a Fly by Simms Taback

What can you do to help yourself infer the meaning of a word?

We were reading stories about George and Martha. We were thinking about how readers infer the meaning of words to better understand what they are reading. We inferred the meanings of these words...

Word	We infer it means	What helped us?
interference	People telling you what to do and saying what you did is wrong	the picture, schema, rereading
touchy	Someone who doesn't like people telling them what to do	schema, rereading
improvements	Things that make it better	schema, picture, rereading, word part
flabbergasted	so mad or shocked or you say "How could you do that!"	picture, schema, rereading
bafers	slippers	picture, "under the table" (words from text)
concentration	thinking hard, needs quiet	picture, schema
offended	mad!	picture, schema
investigate	go find something, like the police	schema, picture
not misunderstanding	fight or argument, not understanding	word parts, schema
distinguished	handsome, wear a hat and a tie and carrying a cane (stick)	words from the book, picture

Now that we know how to infer the meaning of a word, we'll use what we know about what helped us when we read other stories, books, articles and information on the Internet and in newspapers.

figure 3.6 *Students use an anchor chart for inferring the meaning of words they don't know.*

Inferring

Bear Wants More by Karma Wilson
George and Martha Back in Town by James Marshall
George and Martha Encore by James Marshall
George and Martha Round and Round by James Marshall
George and Martha Tons of Fun by James Marshall
George and Martha: The Complete Stories of Two Best Friends by James
   Marshall
The Cow That Went Oink by Bernard Most
The Little Mouse, the Red, Ripe Strawberry, and the Big Hungry Bear by
   Don and Audrey Wood

Older English Language Learners in Real Time

Manuel, Ramon, and Osvaldo: trying to engage this trio of twelve-year-olds in learning is an ongoing challenge. Today's goal is to use informational text and see if they can begin to ask questions based on the illustrations and photographs.

Growing up hasn't been easy for Manuel. At the young age of twelve, he has already spent several years living on the streets in Mexico and doing odd jobs. Adjusting to living in the United States under the watchful eye of his mother is hard for him.

Technology is new to Ramon. He finds using a mouse and a computer very challenging without well-developed fine-motor skills. He has yet to discover video games.

Osvaldo's new glasses give him the look of an intellectual, and he is living up to it. His favorite new word is *hamlet.* "Ask me what it means!" he calls out. Then quickly, he answers his own question: "A small village or group of houses."

What are some good informational books to select for these three as Juli introduces the strategy of asking questions? She starts with a pile of texts that includes two books by Steve Jenkins, *What Do You Do With a Tail Like This?* and *What Do You Do When Something Wants to Eat You?*; a book by Joy Cowley titled *Red-Eyed Tree Frog*; and *The Snake Book, A Breathtaking Close-Up Look at Splendid, Scaly, Slithery Snakes,* a DK Book by Mary Ling and Mary Atkinson.

Juli models using the questions from *Red-Eyed Tree Frog* to guide her thinking. The first question in the book—"What will it eat?"—leads to lots of discussion about what frogs eat. Yuck! These boys definitely have background knowledge about the diets of frogs. The next question is "Do iguanas eat frogs?" There's lots of chatter about iguanas as pets. Evidently, iguanas can exist on dog food. Juli wonders aloud if iguanas might like to eat frogs more than dog food. No one seems to know.

"Will it eat a caterpillar?" the book asks, and the three boys agree that it will. But instead the frog sights a snake and escapes. What does the frog ultimately eat? In the end, he catches and consumes a moth. The boys don't think a moth would taste very good.

After this modeling, the kids each choose a book and use the photographs and illustrations to ask questions. For students at this stage, the idea is to engage them with the text. Juli uses guessing games with yes/no, either/or and who/what/where questions. This draws the boys into the text.

Osvaldo takes a look at the book about snakes and comments, "I want to know about snakes."

"Why?" Manuel asks.

"*Mi mamá* hates snakes!" he replies.

1: Making Connections

Teaching Moves

Start-up/Connection To start, take a picture walk through the book *I Hate English*, drawing students into an open dialog about the illustrations. This will encourage them to draw on their prior knowledge.

Give Information As you read aloud *I Hate English* to students, model making text-to-self connections. Explain the strategy and demonstrate how it applies to the text by thinking aloud, "When I was reading this part, it reminded me of...." Write your connections on a sticky note and post it on an anchor chart.

Active Involvement After the first read-aloud of the book, go through the book again. This time have students share their connections as you read. Encourage them to act out their connections by role playing. As they tell their connections, write each one on a sticky note. Give the sticky note to the student to post on the anchor chart. Students may write their own connections on sticky notes if they are comfortable doing that. See figure 3.7.

Off You Go Provide a collection of predictable books with which the students are familiar. Explain that they will choose books to read with a partner. As they read together, have them write their connections to the story on a page in their strategy application notebook. Tell students that this is just like what they did when they put their connections on the anchor chart. (It is a good idea to model how to use the strategy application notebook before having students begin work.)

2: Asking Questions

Teaching Moves

Start-up/Connection Provide pictures of mice and whales. While students look at the pictures, discuss what they know about mice and whales. Help students understand the unusual nature of the relationship between the mouse and the whale in this story. Then, take a picture walk through the book, drawing

---

Instructional Materials

- *I Hate English* by Ellen Levine
- Anchor chart
- Strategy application notebooks
- Collection of predictable texts at http://www.monroe.lib.in.us/childrens/predict.html Monroe County Public Library, Monroe County, Indiana

Instructional Materials

- Pictures of mice and whales
- *Amos and Boris* by William Steig
- Overhead transparency for anchor chart labeled "Asking Questions: Before, During, and After Reading"
- Strategy application notebooks
- Other books by William Steig (*Shrek!* and *Dr. De Soto*)

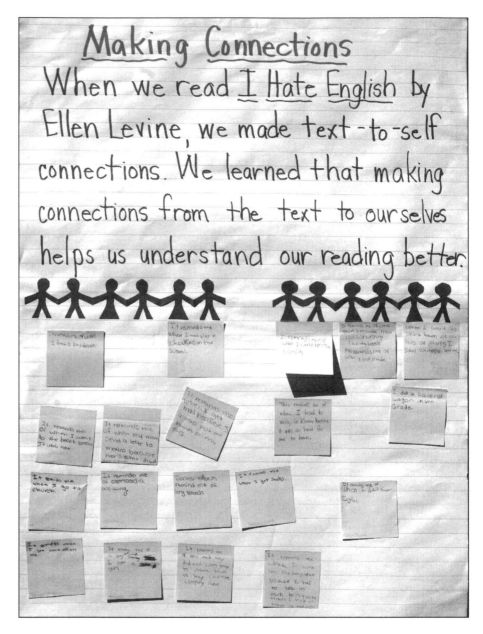

students into an open dialog about the illustrations. This will encourage them to draw on their prior knowledge about mice and whales.

Give Information As you read aloud the book *Amos and Boris* to students, model by asking questions. Explain the questioning strategy and demonstrate how it applies to the text by thinking aloud, "When I was reading this part of the book, I wondered about.... Here's my question...." Write your question on the overhead anchor chart for "Asking Questions."

Asking Questions about *Amos and Boris* by William Steig

Questions Before Reading

Why is the water moving?
Why is the mouse in the boat?
What is the name of the mouse?

Questions During Reading

Who is Amos going to play cards with?
Why is he bringing food?
Can mice swim?
How are they going to save Amos?
Why did the mouse take a trip on the boat?
Why did the whale ask, "What sort of fish are you?"

Questions After Reading

Why did the author ask questions in the story such as, "But what if a
   shark or some big fish turned up?"
Will Amos see his friend Boris again?
What will the mouse do now?

Active Involvement After the first read-aloud of the book, go through the book
again. This time as you read aloud, stop frequently to have students talk to a
partner about their questions. After students have generated questions,
encourage them to share with the whole group. Providing opportunities for
students to talk with a partner and then share with the group encourages oral
language development.

Off You Go Provide a collection of books by William Steig that the students have
not read. Explain that they will work with a partner and choose a book to read.
As they read, have them tell their questions to their partner and then write their
questions and wonderings about the story on a page in their strategy application notebook. Tell students that this is just like what they did when they put
their questions on the anchor chart. Have them organize their questions for
before, during, and after reading. (It is a good idea to model how to use the
strategy application notebook before having students work on their own.)

3: Visualizing—Creating Mental Images

Teaching Moves

Start-up/Connection Provide copies of several poems written by older English
Language Learners. Often student work from the previous year is a good
source. Allow students plenty of time to listen to the poems as you read
aloud. Allow "think time" for students and provide opportunities for them
to talk with each other about the poems. This encourages oral language
development.

Instructional Materials
- Copies of poems writ-
  ten by older students
- Strategy application
  notebooks

Give Information Explain to students that making mental images and visualizing movies in your mind while you read helps readers understand. Share poems that other students have written.

Poems by Helen Vu

I Like Nobody

I like nobody
        I think
                Billy and Joel
                        But they don't
                                And I don't like them
I like nobody
        And nobody likes me
                But Billy and Joel
                        Like me now
                                And I don't
                                        Like them
I LIKE NOBODY
        AND NOBODY LIKES ME

You're the One

I think
You're the one
I try all
My moves
and why
waste my
time

Crazy Minded

I had a book
That took my mind away
And it could be a great book
But I thought it wouldn't do
It went so soon that it
Took my mind so far
Away that I can't find it no more

Baby Sister

I have a baby sister
That likes to drool a lot
She drools everywhere
We go
There is drool there and here

Crazy Pencil on the Run

I had a pencil
That is no ordinary pencil
It talks to me and it moves
All over the place and gets me
In trouble that I didn't do
I say, "It's a crazy pencil on the run."

Active Involvement Tell students that they will choose a poem and draw a visualization for it. Model first by thinking aloud as you draw a visualization of a poem. Then have students give it a try. Encourage conversation about the visualizations as students work. See figures 3.8 and 3.9 for student visualizations of the poem.

Off You Go After students draw their visualizations, have them work with a partner to compare them. Encourage students to talk about the similarities and differences between their visualizations for the same poems. This helps students understand that readers create images as they read and that these images differ from person to person based on their schema and prior knowledge.

figure 3.8 *Casey's visualization of the poem, "Crazy Pencil on the Run," written by Helen Vu.*

figure 3.9 *If we save student writing from year to year, students like Rosita can use texts to apply strategies such as visualizing poetry.*

4: Inferring

Teaching Moves

Start-up/Connection This lesson focuses on using *Just a Dream* by Chris Van Allsburg, but the lesson is easily adapted to any of Van Allsburg's other books. To build background for the story, talk to students about how their family sorts the trash. Also ask what they know about protecting the environment. Explain how people have different opinions about what the future will be like. Find out what students predict will happen in the future. Then take a picture walk through the book, talking about what is happening in the pictures.

Give Information To teach students about inferring at the word stage, read aloud the story, stopping on each page and modeling how you wonder about the meanings of words and phrases as you read. Use the context from the pictures to infer the meanings. For example: "As I'm reading the first page, I'm wondering what the phrase *crumpled up the empty bag* means. So I check the picture and notice that the boy is looking away and that a white paper bag is lying on the ground. I bet he threw it down there. Look how he is standing. He looks upset. I'm going to infer that *crumpled up the empty bag* might mean that when he was finished eating the doughnut, he crushed the bag and threw it on the ground. He didn't even take the time to throw it in the trash can." Be sure to use gestures and point to the places in the picture that helped you infer. Allow talking time. Students can talk to a partner about what they notice and what they infer. Make a chart with three columns labeled "Word or Phrase," "We infer it means," and "What helped us." Write the words *crumpled up* in the first column. Fill in the other two columns as a model for the students.

Instructional Materials

- *Just a Dream* by Chris Van Allsburg
- Other Chris Van Allsburg books such as *Jumanji, The Wreck of the Zephyr, Two Bad Ants,* and *The Polar Express*
- Overhead transparency for anchor chart labeled "What do you do to help yourself infer the meaning of a word you don't know?"
- Strategy application notebooks

Inferring the Meanings of Words and Phrases in *Just a Dream* by Chris Van Allsburg		
Word or Phrase	**We infer it means**	**What helped us**
Crumpled up	You take your hands and squish it hard.	1. look at the picture 2. try doing it ourselves
Sort through	Dig inside—divide it up	1. the words 2. the picture 3. what we already knew about trash
Future	What's going to happen	1. the words 2. what we learned in school about the past, present, and future
His wish came true	What you want, you get it	1. what we already knew about wishes
Dump	Where there is a lot of dirty, smelly trash; you can take your trash there and leave it	1. some of us have been to the dump, and we know how bad it is

Active Involvement Continue reading from the book. As you read each page, stop and let students infer the meaning of unknown words and phrases. Have students add the words and phrases to the chart.

Off You Go Provide other opportunities for students to read books by Chris Van Allsburg. Encourage them to work with a partner, to talk about how they infer the meanings of the unknown words. Have students draw charts in their strategy application notebooks to record the words and phrases whose meanings they are inferring.

Books for Teaching Strategies to Older English Language Learners

Early Production Stage

Making Connections

Grandma and Me at the Flea by Juan Felipe Herrera
Henry's First-Moon Birthday by Lenore Look
I Hate English by Ellen Levine
Just a Minute: a Trickster Tale and *Counting Book* by Yuyi Morales
Work by Ann Morris

Asking Questions

Amos and Boris by William Steig
DK Readers: *Twisters* (Stage 2: Beginning to Read Alone) by Kate Hayden
Red-Eyed Tree Frog by Joy Cowley
What Do You Do When Something Wants to Eat You? by Steve Jenkins
What Do You Do With a Tail Like This? by Steve Jenkins

Visualizing

A Movie in My Pillow by Jorge Argueta
Night of the Gargoyles by Eve Bunting
The Bug in Teacher's Coffee: And Other School Poems by Kalli Dakos
The Color of Us by Karen Katz

Inferring

Jumanji by Chris Van Allsburg
Just a Dream by Chris Van Allsburg
The Polar Express by Chris Van Allsburg
The Stranger by Chris Van Allsburg
The Wreck of the Zephyr by Chris Van Allsburg

SPEECH EMERGENCE

4

Younger English Language Learners in Real Time

Searching for a way to help young English Language Learners synthesize as they read, Outey decides to use retelling to provide a framework for students' thinking.

Viemoll and Vichneath are both reading the Chinese folktale "The Shady Tree." As Outey works with them, she focuses on using retelling as a way to give them a simple framework to synthesize information and check for comprehension.

She has the students do a written retelling of the folktale and assesses their work, using a rubric for fiction retelling. This helps her determine where they are and what she needs to teach next to help them progress. What does she learn about their ability to retell fiction? She notices that they don't have a definite beginning, middle, and ending to their retellings. Also, they sometimes copy material from the text rather than writing in their own words.

Based on her assessment of the students' work, Outey decides these students need more scaffolding to improve their retellings. She introduces another folktale, "The Elves and the Shoemaker." To facilitate their progress in retelling, she adds the concepts of beginning, middle, and ending. She does

figure 4.1 *(above left) Johnny applies strategies independently by reading on the computer.*

figure 4.2 *(above center) Authors like Patricia Placco encourage students' connections.*

figure 4.3 *(above right) Jose thinks about his schema to make connections.*

55

this by teaching them to use transition words: *first, next,* and *last.* After they've read the simple folktale, she helps them orally rehearse their retellings, encouraging them to avoid copying from the text. They take time to think through what they want to say and then frame it with the words *first, next,* and *last.*

Viemoll is the bravest, so she starts. Vichneath follows.

After the oral retellings, Outey introduces written retellings, using a flow map as a graphic organizer. They use a series of three boxes, drawing a picture of the beginning, middle, and ending, one in each box. Then they write a caption for each picture. As they share their retelling flow maps with other students, it is clear that using oral rehearsal and a flow map as a graphic organizer helps them "remember to tell what is important...in a way that makes sense...trying not to tell too much" (Miller 2002).

Lesson Plans for Younger English Language Learners

1: Making Connections

Teaching Moves

Start-up/Connection Hand out several books by Kevin Henkes with which students are already familiar. Give them time to browse through the books. As they are browsing, encourage them to discuss the similarities and differences they notice between the books.

Give Information Explain to students that they will learn about text-to-text connections. Say something such as, "This is when you are reading a book or other text and it reminds you of something you have read before." Choose a "new" text by Kevin Henkes and read it aloud to the students. Model your own text-to-text connections by thinking aloud, writing them on sticky notes, and putting them in the book at the place where you make the connections. Make connections to other texts by Henkes to help students understand how to make connections between texts.

Active Involvement Explain to the students that the similarities they noticed between the books can help them make text-to-text connections. Have students work with a partner to read one of the stories and make text-to-text connections, using the sticky notes to record their connections between the books and mark the text, as in figure 4.4.

Off You Go For independent practice, encourage partner reading with opportunities for retelling to check comprehension. Have students read books from the Kevin Henkes author set and use sticky notes to record their text-to-text connections.

Instructional Materials

- Books by Kevin Henkes (such as *Chrysanthemum; Julius, the Baby of the World; Owen; Wemberly Worried;* and *Chester's Way*)
- Sticky notes

figure 4.4 *Kevin Henkes's books are shown filled with students' connections.*

2: Asking Questions

Teaching Moves

Start-up/Connection Before reading aloud *Apple Pie 4th of July* to the students, take a picture walk through the book to familiarize them with the content. Encourage discussions about the pictures. Model by asking your own questions before reading the text. Record your questions on sticky notes.

Give Information Explain to students that you are going to ask questions about *Apple Pie 4th of July* as you read it aloud. As students listen to the text, model how you ask questions while you read. Use sticky notes to record your questions about the text. Continue asking questions about the story after you finish reading to model for the students. Help them understand that thoughtful readers ask questions before, during, and after they read.

Active Involvement To get students involved in asking questions about *Apple Pie 4th of July*, have them work with you to organize your questions about the story on a "questioning web." Post all the sticky notes with questions on the chart and then work together to categorize them. Then, as a group, choose one

> **Instructional Materials**
> - *Apple Pie 4th of July* by Janet Wong
> - Anchor chart for questioning web
> - Sticky notes

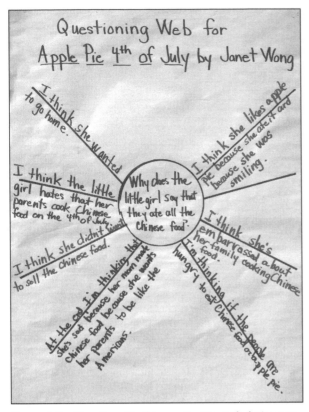

figure 4.5 *We referred to this questioning web during our reading of* Apple Pie 4th of July.

question to write in the middle of the web. Have students help you fill in the web as you model your thinking for them. See the example in figure 4.5.

Off You Go For independent practice, encourage students to construct individual questioning webs for the story *Apple Pie 4th of July*. Remind them that they may include a question from before, during, and after reading and then record their thinking on the web.

3: Visualizing—Creating Mental Images

Teaching Moves

Start-up/Connection Start by saying something such as, "Before we start reading *The Upside Down Boy*, let's take some time to talk about our first day of school." As students begin to describe their first day of school, write the words they use on a large piece of chart paper. Encourage conversation by entering in and prompting if students seem reluctant.

Give Information "Authors, like Juan Felipe Herrera, use descriptive words and details to help us visualize what we are reading, just like the words we wrote on our chart. But it's also our responsibility to create pictures in our minds as we read so that we understand the text." Point out examples of descriptive words from the text.

Active Involvement As you read the text aloud, encourage students to analyze the pictures in the book for details. After reading each page, talk with students about the descriptive words and phrases in the story that help them visualize where it is taking place, what is happening, and what the characters look like. Give students plenty of time to think about the story. Have them talk about which words help them visualize the text. Encourage them to describe their mental images of going to school as much as possible. See student visualizations in figures 4.6 and 4.7.

Off You Go Ask students to draw their visualizations of *The Upside Down Boy* in their strategy application notebooks. When they have finished drawing, hand out copies of the book so that they can compare what they have visualized with the pictures in the text. Encourage students to share with a partner the similarities and differences between their pictures and the ones in the book. This helps them understand that readers create images as they read and that

figure 4.6 *David's visualization of* The Upside Down Boy.

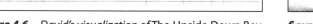

figure 4.7 *Vichneath draws her mental image of the story.*

these images differ from person to person based on their schema and prior knowledge.

4: Inferring

Teaching Moves

Start-up/Connection Help students draw on their prior knowledge about inferring. Start a discussion about what can be inferred from the title of the book, *The Good Luck Cat*, and the illustration of the cat on the front cover. Have students use their prior knowledge about cats to predict the meaning of the title.

Give Information Start by saying something such as, "Today we are going to infer as we read this story. That means we will be 'reading between the lines' to infer what we think the text means. We'll use the two-column chart to record our thinking as we read the text aloud."

Active Involvement As you read the book aloud, think aloud about the places in the text that help you infer the meaning of the story. Write them on one side of the chart. On the other side of the chart, write what you infer. Stop

> **Instructional Materials**
> - *The Good Luck Cat* by Joy Harjo
> - Chart paper for two-column chart labeled "What the Text Says / What We Infer"

frequently and provide time for students to talk with a partner about the story. As you continue, have them contribute their own inferences for the chart.

What We Infer from *The Good Luck Cat* by Joy Harjo	
What the text says	**What we infer**
"Woogie is a good luck cat."	We infer that you are lucky if you have this cat.
"the spring powwow"	She's a Native American.
"But Woogie's 9 lives went fast."	She had a lot of problems.
"Cats are born to hunt."	They like to catch mice, birds, and lizards.
"For 4 days I missed my stripedy cat."	She feels sad that Woogie is gone.
"Her ear was bitten in half."	Woogie had been fighting.

Off You Go Allow students to read other stories with a partner. Provide sticky notes for them to use to mark the places in the text that help them infer. Encourage them to orally share their thinking with each other about where in the text they find the information that helps them with their inferences.

5: Determining Importance in Nonfiction

Teaching Moves

Start-up/Connection To provide comprehensible input about nonfiction conventions, provide a wide variety of nonfiction texts that students can look through and read. Encourage them to talk with each other about what they notice in the texts that helps them understand the content. As our students look through the nonfiction books, they usually point out specific conventions such as the table of contents, the glossary, and the chapter headings. Juli encouraged one group of students by saying, "Let's take a look at this book and see what you notice about dolphins."

"There's a glossary," Loren said.

Juli asked, "What in the world is a glossary? Anybody know?"

"Information about the words from the book," Vanessa volunteered.

"Okay," Juli continued. "Somebody said it's like a little tiny dictionary for your book. Do you like that? A little dictionary for your book."

The discussion about informational text features continued as students noticed the table of contents, chapter headings, and italic used for important words, pictures and captions.

When there was confusion about why killer whales were pictured in a book about dolphins, Juli clarified by saying, "The reason the killer whales are in this book is that although we call them killer whales, they are actually in the dolphin family. That's an amazing fact that you'll find out as you read this book with a partner." Some suggested texts for this stage are Step Into

---

Instructional Materials

- Nonfiction texts that explicitly show nonfiction conventions

  Dolphins by Victoria St. John

  Finding the Titanic by Robert D. Ballard

  Grade-level textbooks

  Humphrey, The Lost Whale, a True Story by Wendy Tokuda and Richard Hall

  Hungry, Hungry Sharks by Joanne Cole

  Ice Mummy: The Discovery of a 5,000-Year-Old Man by Mark Dubowski and Cathy East Dubowski

  National Geographic Kids magazine

  Sea Turtles by Stanley L. Swartz

  The Moon Book by Gail Gibbons

- Nonfiction conventions booklets (Harvey and Goudvis 2000 and Miller 2002)

Reading books such as *Hungry, Hungry, Sharks* by Joanne Cole, Hello Reader books such as *Finding the Titanic* by Robert D. Ballard, Let's Read and Find Out About Science books such as *How Mountains Are Made,* books from Gail Gibbons such as *The Moon Book,* magazines such as *National Geographic Explorer,* and other accessible nonfiction texts.

Give Information Explain to students that they will make a nonfiction conventions booklet. This book-let is made up of six sheets of 8½-by-11-inch paper. The paper is folded over and stapled together with a construction paper cover. Hand out the booklets and have students write the title "Nonfiction Conventions" and decorate the cover. Before they decorate, discuss the difference between fiction and nonfiction and explain that this booklet is only for nonfiction conventions. This helps students stay on task as they decorate the booklets. See figure 4.8.

Active Involvement Select nonfiction conventions that are important for the students to know. Teach one each day by reading aloud a book that has a clear example of that convention. As you read the book, stop and have students talk to a partner about what helps them understand the content. Emphasize how the nonfiction convention you are teaching helps you understand the text. Have students include an example of the nonfiction convention on a page in their notebooks. Here are some examples of books that explicitly demonstrate nonfiction conventions:

figure 4.8 *Models of nonfiction convention booklets scaffold the concept for students.*

Table of Contents—*Dolphins* by Victoria St. John
Index—grade-level textbooks
Glossary—*Sea Turtles* by Stanley L. Swartz
Charts and diagrams—*The Moon Book* by Gail Gibbons
Maps—*Humphrey, The Lost Whale, a True Story* by Wendy Tokuda and Richard Hall
Photographs—*Finding the Titanic* by Robert D. Ballard
Captions—*Ice Mummy: The Discovery of a 5,000-Year-Old Man* by Mark Dubowski and Cathy East Dubowski
Comparisons—*Hungry, Hungry Sharks* by Joanna Cole
Cutaways—*National Geographic Kids* magazine

Off You Go Have students save several pages at the back of their nonfiction conventions booklet to record other nonfiction conventions they discover as they read with their partners. Have them share their discoveries with the whole group so others can talk about how they think the convention helps them understand the text.

6: Synthesizing

Teaching Moves

Start-up/Connection Synthesizing is probably the most complex comprehension strategy. We didn't actually teach it until we began doing inquiry projects with our students. The process of inquiry involves developing a conjecture and then revising and changing it by doing research. We find that our students need to understand how their thinking changes as they research and discover new information, and that this is a result of synthesizing.

We also realized that we needed to introduce the idea of synthesizing before they began inquiry so that they were comfortable with the strategy. We created a synthesizing frame to act as a scaffold for their thinking. To gradually release responsibility, we first use the frame to introduce synthesizing with literature. As they become more proficient, we encourage them to use the frame to synthesize in other areas such as science and history. The question we always want them to keep in mind is, How is my thinking changing? When we need additional clarification and support for our thinking about synthesizing, we turn to *Strategies That Work* by Harvey and Goudvis, page 143, and *Reading with Meaning* by Debbie Miller, starting with page 158.

To activate students' prior knowledge, draw them into a conversation about what they know about bats. Read *Bats* by Gail Gibbons to provide comprehensible input about bats. Use the context from the story *Stellaluna* to help students infer the meaning of the new vocabulary they will encounter as they read along with you. It's important for them to know the meaning of words such as *sultry, crooned, clutched, spied,* and *limp*. Write a sentence containing vocabulary that needs to be clarified on chart paper. For example: "In a warm and sultry forest, far, far away, there once lived a mother fruit bat and her new baby." Use the pictures, what the text says, and what students already know about forests (their schema) to infer the meaning of the word *sultry*. See the chart below.

Vocabulary That Needs to Be Clarified in *Stellaluna* by Janell Cannon		
Vocabulary We Need to Clarify	**Words from the Text**	**What We Think (Infer) It Means**
Sultry	"In a warm and sultry forest, far, far away, there once lived a mother fruit bat and her new baby."	We think it means something about the weather because it says *warm*. Maybe it means wet weather?

Give Information Help students understand that synthesizing is about keeping track of "how your thinking changes" as you read. The question we want them to think about is, How has my thinking changed based on what I am reading? Having a frame for their thinking about synthesizing scaffolds the task for them. For example: "Before I start reading, I'm thinking the book

Stellaluna is about bats and why they fly at night. So as I read the book, I'm going to keep track of how my thinking changes."

Synthesizing Frame

Before we started reading ____, I was thinking that ____.
Then when we first started reading, I thought it was going to be about
    ____ because ____.
But then we read something different about ____.
So I'm changing my thinking because _____.

Active Involvement Give students sticky notes to use to indicate the places in the story where their thinking changes. As you read the story together, model how you highlight where your thinking changes. Have students talk with their partners about what they notice. Have them use sticky notes to mark where their thinking changes. Use the synthesizing frame to write your synthesis on chart paper to serve as a model. Have them write their synthesis in their strategy application notebooks and then share with the group. See figures 4.9 and 4.10 for examples.

Off You Go Provide opportunities for students to read other books. Encourage them to work with a partner and talk about where in the text their thinking changes. They can do additional synthesizing by using the synthesis frame in their strategy application notebooks.

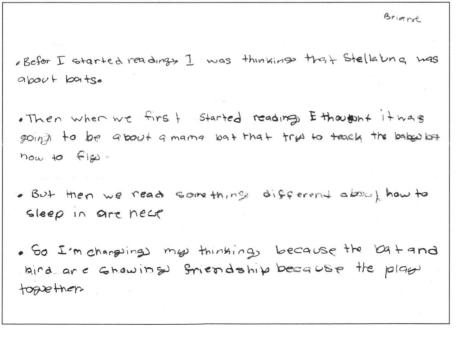

Briane

• Befor I started reading, I was thinking that Stellaluna was about bats.

• Then when we first started reading I thought it was going to be about a mama bat that tryd to teach the baby bat how to fly.

• But then we read something different about how to sleep in are neck

• So I'm changing my thinking because the bat and bird are showing friendship because the play together.

figure 4.9 *Briane changed her thinking several times while reading* Stellaluna.

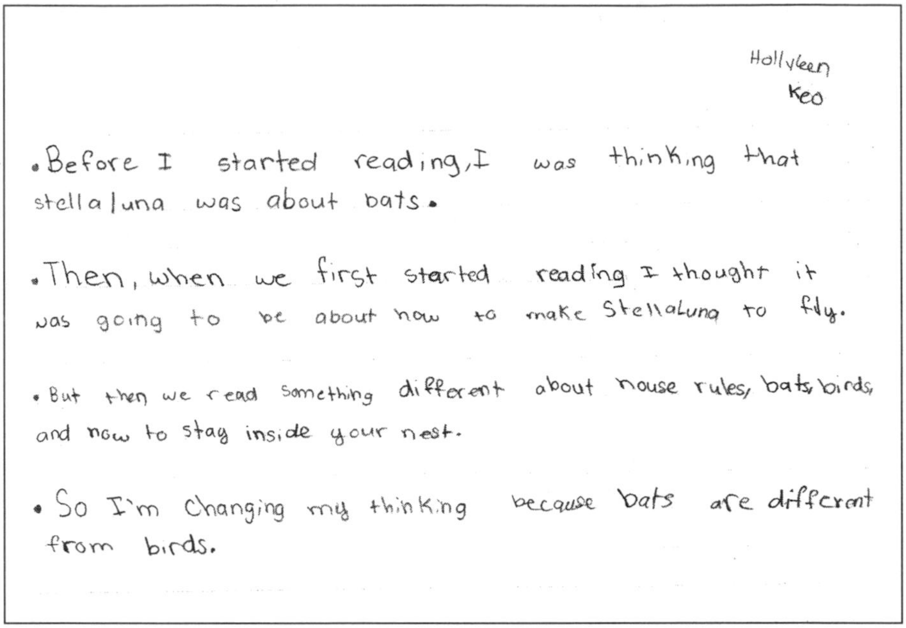

figure 4.10 *Hollyleen kept track of her thinking when she used a synthesizing frame.*

> Hollyleen
> Keo
>
> • Before I started reading, I was thinking that stellaluna was about bats.
>
> • Then, when we first started reading I thought it was going to be about how to make Stellaluna to fly.
>
> • But then we read something different about house rules, bats, birds, and how to stay inside your nest.
>
> • So I'm changing my thinking because bats are different from birds.

Books for Teaching Strategies to Younger English Language Learners

Speech Emergence Stage

Making Connections

Amelia's Road by Linda Altman
Books by Kevin Henkes
My Name Is Yoon by Helen Recorvitz
Too Many Tamales by Gary Soto
Dim Sum for Everyone by Grace Lin

Asking Questions

Apple Pie 4th of July by Janet Wong
Spiders' Secrets, DK Readers by Richard Platt
What Lives in a Shell? by Kathleen Weidner Zoehfeld
What Makes Day and Night? by Franklin Branley
Mama and Papa Have a Store by Amelia Lau Carling

Visualizing

The Upside Down Boy by Juan Felipe Herrera
Abuela by Arthur Dorros
Calling the Doves by Juan Felipe Herrera
Sky Scrape/City Scape, Poems of City Life selected by Jane Yolen
This Is the House That Jack Built by Simms Taback

Inferring

Click, Clack, Moo: Cows That Type by Doreen Cronin
Juan Bobo—Four Folktales from Puerto Rico retold by Carmen
　Bernier-Grand
The Good Luck Cat by Joy Harjo
Liang and the Magic Paint Brush by Hitz Demi
The Legend of the Hummingbird: A Tale from Puerto Rico by Michael
　Rose Ramirez

Determining Importance in Nonfiction

National Geographic Kids magazine
Finding the Titanic (Hello Reader series) by Robert D. Ballard
How Mountains Are Made (Let's Read and Find Out About Science) by
　Kathleen Weidner Zoehfeld
Hungry, Hungry Sharks (Step Into Reading Books) by Joanne Cole
The Moon Book by Gail Gibbons

Synthesizing

Big Moon Tortilla by Joy Cowley
Napí by Antonio Ramírez
Stellaluna by Janell Cannon
The Great Kapok Tree by Lynne Cherry
The Trip Back Home by Janet Wong

Older English Language Learners in Real Time

Students are working on learning to infer, and the table for the small-group lesson is covered with cartoons. Kids are reading from "Garfield," "Calvin and Hobbes," and several books filled with cartoons from "The Far Side" by Gary Larsen. What has this got to do with reading comprehension strategies? Because our students are English Language Learners, visuals, particularly cartoons, are well suited to teaching about inferring. It's a reasonable assumption that "a picture is worth a thousand words," and that is especially true for our students. Using cartoons, along with other visuals such as charts, graphics, and photographs, also adds context to the strategy tasks we ask our students to do and facilitates the use of oral language. It encourages our students to use higher-level thinking such as inferring while their vocabularies may still be limited. But there's another angle to using cartoons to teach strategies. According to Outey, "I myself have a hard time inferring from cartoons. So much of what makes cartoons funny comes from the culture. Sometimes, even when someone explains the cartoon to me, I still don't see the humor. So another benefit of using cartoons to teach inferring is that you are also teaching culture by teaching students what makes a cartoon funny." But when everyone does "get it," the combination of laughter and learning is unbeatable.

This group of five eleven- and twelve-year-olds is totally engaged. Juli's plan is to use this material to get kids to think about inferring, to practice connecting their prior knowledge to what they are reading and make meaning beyond what is directly stated. As they read another text together, Juli will link back, connecting it to what they learned about how to infer using the cartoons. She's gradually releasing the responsibility because she wants them to become independent in the use of this comprehension strategy—able to do it on their own.

As Juli begins the study of inferring, she asks the kids, "What do you know about how to infer?" There are lots of responses, so we write them on a sheet of chart paper titled "What is inferring?"

"Inferring is predicting."

"I infer when I don't know what is happening."

"If I want to infer, I think."

"We did that last year, and my teacher taught us."

"It's what you do at the end of the story when the guy disappears and you don't know if he has moved or died."

Then Juli shares what she knows about inferring and adds it to the chart paper:

- Inferring is connecting prior knowledge (what you already know) to what you are reading or learning to create meaning beyond what is directly stated.
- "Inferring is about reading faces, reading body language, reading expressions, and reading tone as well as reading text" (Harvey and Goudvis 2000, p. 105).

There is lots of conversation in this small group about what's happening in the pictures and what each cartoon means. Students share inferences with each other. Over several days, the small group talks, discusses, agrees, and disagrees about these cartoons. All the while, they practice how to infer. One question that arises is "What is a reasonable assumption about the meaning that is not directly stated?" Juli finds that having kids respond using the word *because* means their thinking is more focused and reasonable. It helps them back up their inferences with evidence.

One of the students' favorite cartoons shows a man standing beside a very tall building and looking down at a broken stool. Above him, a piano is falling toward the ground. The kids infer independently, write down their inferences, and then share them with the small group.

"I can infer that the man is looking at the chair and not the piano."

"I infer that the man plays the piano but if he looks up he is going to get hit with the piano because they dropped it down."

"I infer that someone hates the man and he wants to kill him."

"I infer that the man is wondering where is the piano because it is not on the floor."

For this small group, cartoons turn out to be a great way to get plenty of practice inferring and, at the same time, have some fun. For these students, cartoons are important because they encourage higher-level thinking, as well as inferring, while limiting the amount of text.

Lesson Plans for Older English Language Learners

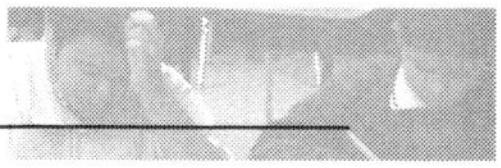

1: Making Connections

Teaching Moves

Start-up/Connection Hand out several books by Patricia Polacco with which students are already familiar. Give them time to browse through the books. As they browse, encourage them to discuss the similarities and differences they notice between the books.

Give Information Explain to students that they will learn about text-to-text connections. Say something such as, "This is when you are reading a book or other text and it reminds you of something you have read before." Choose a "new" text by Patricia Polacco and read it aloud to the students. Model your own text-to-text connections by thinking aloud, writing them on a sticky note, and putting them in the book at the places where you make the connections. Make connections to other texts by Polacco to help students understand how to make text-to-text connections.

Active Involvement To get students involved in making text-to-text connections between the books in the Patricia Polacco author set, explain that the similarities they noticed between the books can help them make text-to-text connections. Have students work with a partner to read one of the stories together and make text-to-text connections using the sticky notes to record their connections and mark the book as in figure 4.11.

Off You Go For independent practice, encourage solo reading with interactive comprehension checks. Have students reread books from the Patricia Polacco author set on their own and use sticky notes to record their text-to-text connections.

Instructional Materials

- Books by Patricia Polacco (such as *Thunder Cake, Chicken Sunday, Mrs. Katz and Tush, The Keeping Quilt, Mrs. Mack,* and *My Rotten Red-Headed Older Brother*)
- Sticky notes

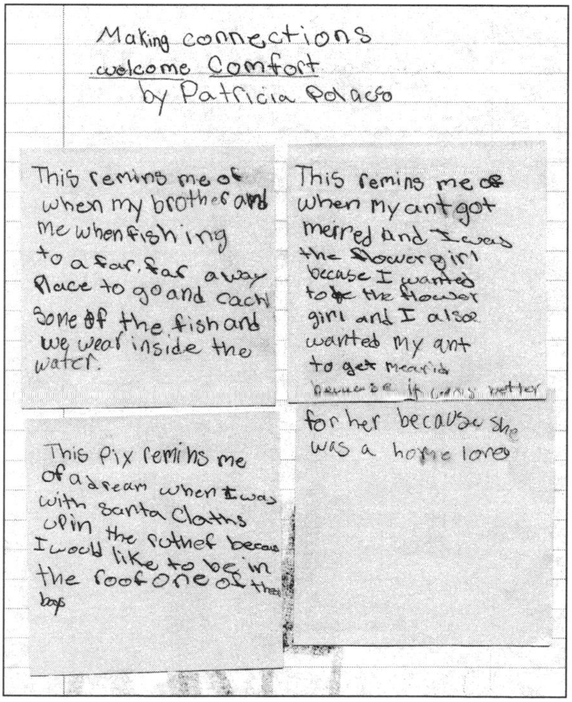

figure 4.11 *Rosa made connections to a Patricia Polacco book during a lesson.*

2: Asking Questions

Teaching Moves

Start-up/Connection Before reading aloud *The Name Jar* to the students, take a picture walk through the book to familiarize them with the content. Encourage discussions about the pictures. Model by asking your own questions before reading the text. Record your questions on sticky notes.

Give Information Explain to students that you are going to ask questions about *The Name Jar* as you read it aloud. As students listen to the text, model how you ask questions while you read. Use sticky notes to record your questions about the text. Continue asking questions about the story after you finish reading to model for the students. Help them understand that good readers ask questions before, during, and after they read.

Active Involvement To get students involved in asking questions about *The Name Jar,* have them work with you to organize your questions about the story on a "questioning web." Post all the sticky notes with questions on the chart and then work together to categorize them. Then, as a group, choose one question to write in the middle of the web. Have students help you fill in the web as you model your thinking for them. See figure 4.12.

Off You Go For independent practice, encourage students to construct individual questioning webs for *The Name Jar.* Remind them that they should include questions from before, during, and after reading and then select one question for the web.

3: Visualizing—Creating Mental Images

Teaching Moves

Start-up/Connection Start with something such as, "Let's start today by talking about hair. Everyone has hair, and everyone has good hair days and bad hair days. I'll start. My hair is short and straight, and sometimes it's thick and sticks out like straw and sometimes it's thin and sticks to my head. So on the chart titled 'Hair,' I'm going to write the words I used to describe my hair: *short, straight, thick, sticks out like straw, thin,* and *sticks to my head.* Who wants to go next?" Encourage students to enter in by prompting, if necessary.

Give Information "Authors, such as Sandra Cisneros, use descriptive words and details to help us visualize what we are reading. But it's also our responsibility to create pictures in our minds as we read so that we understand the text."

Active Involvement There are two different versions of the same text in this lesson. The first one is "Hairs," an excerpt from *The House on Mango Street.* It

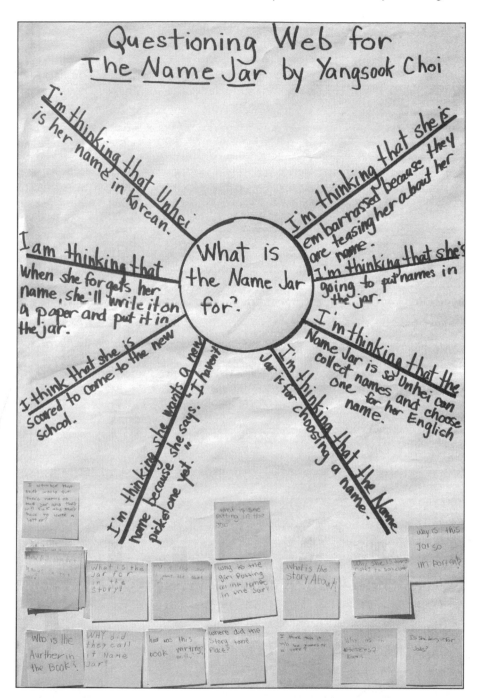

figure 4.12   *The questioning web shows how students in the small group think about the question, "What is the Name Jar for?"*

Hairs

Everybody in our family has different hair. My Papa's hair is like a broom, all up in the air. And me, my hair is lazy. It never obeys barrettes or bands. Carlos' hair is thick and straight. He doesn't need to comb it. Nenny's hair is slippery—slides out of your hand. And Kiki, who is the youngest, has hair like fur.

But my mother's hair, my mother's hair, like little rosettes, like little candy circles all curly and pretty because she pinned it in pincurls all day, sweet to put your nose into when she is holding you, holding you and you feel safe, is the warm smell of bread before you bake it, is the

6   Sandra Cisneros

figure 4.13   Nestor decides how to create a mental image of "My Papa's hair is like a broom" after reading the chapter "Hairs."

figure 4.14   Mary visualized the text to determine how to represent this excerpt from The House on Mango Street.

does not contain any illustrations. Read this short selection to students first. As you read, allow time for students to think about the text. Encourage conversation about what they visualize by modeling first and then asking them to describe their mental images.

Off You Go Ask students to draw their visualizations of the excerpt "Hairs" in their strategy application notebooks. When they have finished drawing, hand out copies of the picture book *Hairs/Pelitos* so they can compare what they have visualized with the pictures in the text, as in figures 4.13 and 4.14. Encourage students to share with a partner the similarities and differences between their pictures and the ones in the book. This helps them understand that readers create images as they read and that these images differ from person to person based on their schema and prior knowledge.

4: Inferring

Teaching Moves

Start-up/Connection Provide background knowledge for students before reading aloud by having them preview pages 12 and 13 from the book *Dateline: Troy* and write down

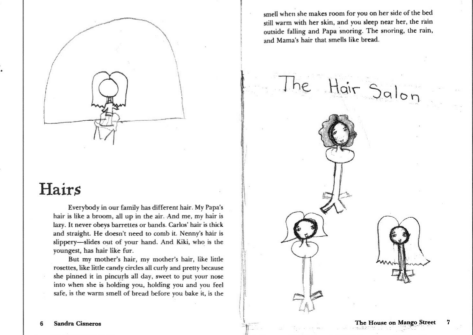

Hairs

Everybody in our family has different hair. My Papa's hair is like a broom, all up in the air. And me, my hair is lazy. It never obeys barrettes or bands. Carlos' hair is thick and straight. He doesn't need to comb it. Nenny's hair is slippery—slides out of your hand. And Kiki, who is the youngest, has hair like fur.

But my mother's hair, my mother's hair, like little rosettes, like little candy circles all curly and pretty because she pinned it in pincurls all day, sweet to put your nose into when she is holding you, holding you and you feel safe, is the warm smell of bread before you bake it, is the

6   Sandra Cisneros

smell when she makes room for you on her side of the bed still warm with her skin, and you sleep near her, the rain outside falling and Papa snoring. The snoring, the rain, and Mama's hair that smells like bread.

The Hair Salon

The House on Mango Street   7

words for which they need clarification in their strategy application note-books. Model how to infer the meaning of unknown words by thinking aloud. For example: "On page 12, I'm not sure about what the word *herdsman* means. I think that it has something to do with animals, because a herd is like a flock of sheep. I also know part of the word—*man*. So maybe it means 'a man who has sheep or animals'?"

Give Information "Today we are going to be inferring as we read a retelling from the Trojan War and a newspaper article from the book *Dateline: Troy*. That means we will be reading between the lines to infer the connection between the selection about Hecuba and Priam and their baby, Paris, and the recent newspaper article 'Newborn Found in Dumpster,' about the baby found in a Dumpster. We also want to see if we can make a connection between this selection and what we have been learning about ancient Greece in history." Use the three-column chart to record your thinking as you read the text aloud.

Instructional Materials
- *Dateline: Troy* by Paul Fleischman
- Overhead transparency for three-column chart labeled "Picture or Quote from the Text/Inference/My Personal Response"
- Strategy application notebooks

Inferring from *Dateline: Troy* by Paul Fleischman		
Picture or Quote from the Text	**Inference**	**My Personal Response**
The myth says, "Priam at last took the baby from her arms, but couldn't bring himself to kill him."	Priam is not going to kill the baby. He will try to save him.	We think that sometimes when babies are born, it is hard for their families to keep them.
The newspaper article says that a newborn infant found in a Dumpster was in good condition.	If the baby was in good condition and it was in the Dumpster, then someone must have been taking care of the baby.	If you have a baby and you can't keep it, you should take it to the fire station or the hospital so that they can check it and find a home.
In the myth the herdsman leaves the baby to die and comes back five days later and a bear is taking care of him.	The bear must have magic powers to be able to take care of a baby.	This was a very lucky baby. We think a bear would usually eat a baby it found, not take care of it.

Active Involvement As you read, encourage students to make their own connections between the Greek myth, the newspaper article, and/or what they learned about Greece in history. Promote oral language development by having students use conversation starters such as, "I think...," "Maybe it means...," "I'm guessing that...," and "I predict..." (Harvey and Goudvis 2000, p. 277). Have them use the three-column chart to record their thinking and their inferences.

Off You Go Provide other opportunities for students to work in pairs to read additional myths and newspaper articles from the book. Have students use the three-column chart as a model and record their thinking and their inferences. Be sure they have opportunities to orally share their thinking with each other.

5: Determining Importance in Nonfiction

Teaching Moves

Start-up/Connection To provide comprehensible input about nonfiction text, provide a wide variety of nonfiction texts that students can look through and read. Encourage them to talk with each other about what they notice in the texts that helps them understand the content. Some suggested texts for this stage: *The Moon Book* by Gail Gibbons includes good examples of diagrams on the pages about phases of the moon. Joanna Cole's *Magic School Bus: On the Ocean Floor* contains a wide variety of captions and labels throughout the book. *The International Space Station* by Franklyn Branley, from the Let's-Read-And-Find-Out Science series, includes a blueprint of the station and an illustration comparing the size of a thirty-foot building and the space station.

Before making the texts available to the students, be sure to evaluate whether or not the illustrations will appeal to older students.

Give Information Explain to students that they will be creating a section in their strategy application notebooks for "I wonder. . ." pages. These pages are a place for them to write all the things that they wonder about. It can give them ideas for research and inquiry as well as help them with their nonfiction writing. Have students count off ten pages in their notebooks and provide sticky tabs for them to mark the pages with the title "I wonder. . . ." Model for the students by using your own strategy application notebook to show them how you tabbed your "I wonder. . ." pages and what you write on them.

Active Involvement To draw the students into a discussion about wondering, read aloud the book *All About Rattlesnakes* by Jim Arnosky. It begins with the question, "Have you ever wondered about rattlesnakes?" and then lists several questions about them. At the bottom of the first page, it tells the readers that the book will answer those questions. Write the questions on a chart. As you read the book, stop and point out answers to the questions when you come to them. Write the answers on the chart. Provide frequent opportunities for students to stop and talk about what they wonder and answers to the questions. Add their wonderings, questions, and the answers they find to the chart.

Henry wonders about rattlesnakes:

I wonder how they have babies.
I wonder how they find their home.
I wonder if they have bones.
I wonder how snakes move straight.
I wonder how big their fangs are.

Instructional Materials

- Nonfiction texts that encourage students to wonder
- *All About Rattlesnakes* by Jim Arnosky
- Overhead transparency for "I wonder..." chart
- "Wonder pages" in strategy application notebooks (Harvey 1998, p. 16)

I wonder how it gets its venom.
I wonder how they shed their old skin and get their new skin.

Rosa wonders about rattlesnakes:

I wonder if they hang from trees like the snakes in Mexico.
I wonder why they coil up.
I wonder why they shake their tails.
I wonder if rattlesnakes have teeth.

Patty wonders about rattlesnakes:

I wonder how long they can be.
I wonder where they have their poison.
I wonder, if the animal they want to eat is big, can they still eat the animal?

Off You Go As students read additional nonfiction texts, have them use their strategy application notebooks to record their wonderings, questions, and any answers they find.

Instructional Materials

- *Tomás and the Library Lady* **by Pat Mora**
- **Overhead transparency for synthesizing-frame anchor chart**
- **Strategy application notebooks**

6: Synthesizing

Teaching Moves

Start-up/Connection: To activate students' prior knowledge, draw them in to a conversation about the library. Talk about the school library and the public library and their similarities and differences. Encourage students to share their experiences in the library and with librarians.

Give Information: Show students the synthesizing frame they will be using as you read with them. Explain that using the synthesizing frame means that you are aware of how your thinking changes when you are reading. The frame serves as a model to help you write down what you are thinking.

Synthesizing Frame

Before I started reading, I was thinking that *Tomás and the Library Lady* was about...
When I first started reading, I thought it was going to be about...
    because I read...
But then I read something different...so I changed my thinking...
Now my synthesis has changed because...

Explain that the question we want them to think about is, "How has my thinking changed based on what I am reading?" Having a frame for their thinking about synthesizing scaffolds the task for them. Model your thinking for them by using the frame. As you read together, show them how you determine where in the story your thinking changes.

Active Involvement Have the students do their own synthesizing frames as you read the story aloud. Make copies of the story available for the students. Have them talk with a partner and indicate the places in the story where their thinking changes. As you read together, model how you highlight where your thinking changes. Use the synthesizing frame to write your synthesis on an overhead transparency. Have them use the frame to write their synthesis in their strategy application notebooks.

Juli's Synthesizing Frame for Tomás and the Library Lady

Before I started reading, I was thinking that *Tomás and the Library Lady* was about a little boy who gets books at the library and forgets to take them back.

When I first started reading, I thought it was going to be about picking fruit in Iowa, because I read that Tomás and his family are driving to Iowa to pick fruit again.

But then I read something different about Papá Grande, who likes to tell stories, so I changed my thinking because Papá Grande tells Tomás that there are lots more stories at the library.

My synthesis has changed because now I'm thinking that Tomás is going to go to the library and check out books so that he can read many more stories. I think he is going to become an excellent reader.

Off You Go Provide opportunities for students to read other biographical books. Encourage them to work with a partner and talk about where their thinking changes. They can do additional synthesizing by using the synthesis frame to write in their strategy application notebooks.

Books for Teaching Strategies to Older English Language Learners

Speech Emergence Stage

Making Connections

Books by Patricia Polacco (such as *Thunder Cake, Chicken Sunday, Mrs. Katz and Tush, The Keeping Quilt, Mrs. Mack, My Rotten Red-Headed Older Brother*)
I Love Saturdays y domingos by Alma Flor Ada

Asking Questions

The Name Jar by Yangsook Choi
MLB Home Run Heroes, DK Readers by James Buckley Jr.
The Planets by Gail Gibbons
The Planets in Our Solar System (Let's-Read-and-Find-Out Science) by Franklyn Branley

Titanic: The Disaster That Shocked the World!, DK Readers by
  Mark Dubowski

Visualizing

"Hairs"—Chapter 2 from *The House on Mango Street* by
  Sandra Cisneros
beast feast: poems by Douglas Florian
Hairs/Pelitos by Sandra Cisneros
lizards, frogs, and polliwogs by Douglas Florian
Confetti: Poems for Children by Pat Mora

Inferring

Abuela's Weave by Omar S. Castaneda
Nine-in-One, Grr! Grr! A Folktale from the Hmong People of Laos by
  Blia Xiong and Nancy Hom
The Firekeeper's Son by Linda Sue Park
Dateline: Troy by Paul Fleischmann
The Journey of the Tunuri and the Blue Deer: A Huichol Indian Story by
  James Endredy

Determining Importance in Nonfiction

All About Rattlesnakes by Jim Arnosky
All About Sharks by Jim Arnosky
Magic School Bus: Inside the Earth by Joanna Cole
Magic Tree House Research Guides: Ancient Greece and the Olympics
  by Mary Pope Osborne
Surprising Sharks by Nicola Davies

Synthesizing

Fortune Cookie Fortunes by Grace Lin
How My Parents Learned to Eat by Ina R. Friedman
In the Space of the Sky by Richard Lewis
Xochiti and the Flowers by Jorge Argueta
Tomás and the Library Lady by Pat Mora

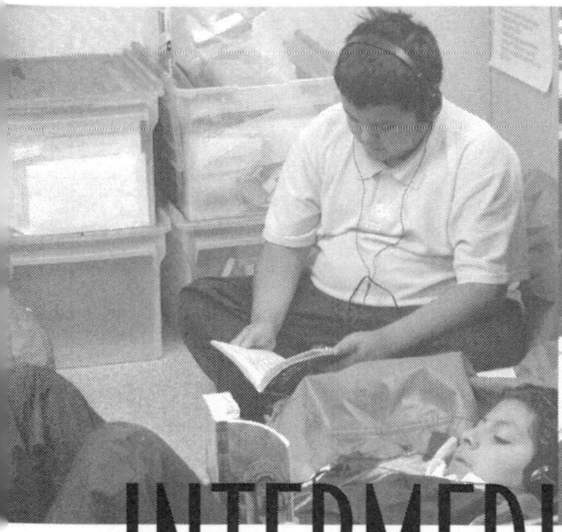

INTERMEDIATE

5

All students benefit from opportunities to use comprehensible input to build background, but for English Language Learners, it is a necessity. It is important to present information in a way that students can understand, keeping in mind their language development needs, linguistic and cultural backgrounds, and educational experiences. To help students comprehend as we teach, new information is tied to their backgrounds and experiences to scaffold their acquisition of language and strategies. This is as important for students at the intermediate and advanced stages as it is for students at beginning stages. As students' oral language develops and the level of difficulty of the text increases, we keep instructional scaffolds such as building background in place. This helps them access their prior knowledge to make connections between what they already know and what they are learning in all content areas. The intermediate and advanced lessons in this book use students' personal experiences and their schema—knowledge of the world—as a basis for understanding, learning, and remembering what they are learning.

As the level of content and concepts increases, determining if students know something about the topic and whether what they know is correct becomes an issue. One helpful resource is *Tools for Teaching Content Literacy* by Janet Allen. It includes a variety of ways to help students organize what they are learning in content areas. The book includes several variations on traditional KWL charts. *K* is for what you already know about a topic, *W* is for

figure 5.1 *(above left) Henry and Nestor listen to books on tape to practice applying strategies during independent reading.*

figure 5.2 *(above center) We often give students like Rosita, Mary, Nayeli, and Drina time to talk with a partner during small groups.*

figure 5.3 *(above right) Nestor and Henry work in a small group to support their thinking about strategies.*

what you wonder about the topic, and *L* is for what you learned about a topic as you studied it. One suggestion is B-K-W-L-Q (*B* for building background knowledge and *Q* for new questions that arise after the initial reading and before further reading and research).

Younger English Language Learners in Real Time

Learning academic content becomes more and more important as students progress through school, so selecting text for this lesson was a challenge. Juli wanted to find informational text that included many text features such as a table of contents, glossary, index, and chapter headings. English Language Learners at this stage need to learn how to read text in content areas, and informational text with lots of text features helps develop content literacy.

Juli also wanted to be able to model text-to-text connections for kids across a variety of genres (poetry, informational, and narrative text) by thinking aloud about her own text-to-text connections as she read. She searched the topic of environmental concerns and focused on dolphins and issues about dolphin-safe tuna. She chose two poems written by a fifth-grade student, a leveled reader titled *Dolphins* by Victoria St. John, a book from the Smithsonian Institution called *Dolphin's First Day: The Story of a Bottlenose Dolphin* by Kathleen Weidner Zoehfeld, and an Internet WebQuest, "Dolphin Safe Tuna."

She sat at the small table with four students whose primary language was Spanish. "Today we are going to make connections," she said. "You know about three different kinds of connections. You know about...."

"Text-to-text," Vanessa finished.

Juli added, "When you're reading something...."

"Text-to-self," Daniel responded.

"Which is when it reminds you of something that happened to you," Juli said, "and text to...."

"World," Jose chimed in.

Juli continued, "Text to world—something that happens in the world, like maybe you see a movie or you hear about something on the news."

Daniel expanded on the idea of text-to-world connections. "It's something like you see a movie and you remember something that happened in the movie when you are reading."

"Exactly," Juli responded. "These are things that good readers do. Making connections is something that good readers do. It helps them understand what they read. We're going to start today by reading a poem about dolphins. It was written by a girl from North Carolina. She's in fifth grade, and she wrote this poem. To help you remember about making connections, I'm giving you a 'making connections' bookmark. You choose the one you would like. You can use the bookmark to keep your place, and you can write your connections on it as you read. Here we go. Let's read the poem 'Dolphins.'"

Juli and her four students made their connections as they did shared reading with two poems. Next, Juli handed out the leveled informational text *Dolphins*. "Here's the book we're going to read about dolphins. It's an informational book. We're also going to read *Dolphin's First Day: The Story of a Bottlenose Dolphin* on another day, and we're going to read like Vanessa did on the Internet about dolphins. We'll be finding out that they might be in danger. We'll have a lot of reading about dolphins to help us make text-to-text connections, connections from things we've read to things we're reading."

As students turned to buddy read the text with their partners, the sound of kids making connections filled the small space. Goal accomplished!

Lesson Plans for Younger English Language Learners

1: Making Connections

Teaching Moves

Start-up/Connection

- Ask a question to elicit students' prior knowledge about dolphins.
- Have students share their experiences with dolphins.
- Brainstorm a variety of characteristics about dolphins, such as habitat, food, and physical description. Include students' experiences and what they know through other means such as TV, movies, the Internet, and cultural connections.
- With students' input, draw a graphic organizer to put their contributions in categories. We suggest the B-K-W-L-Q chart from Janet Allen's *Tools for Teaching Content Literacy*.
- If necessary, provide comprehensible input about the topic: Internet Web sites and WebQuests, other books (*Dolphin's First Day: The Story of a Bottlenose Dolphin* by Kathleen Weidner Zoehfeld and *Dolphins and Sharks: Magic Tree House Research Guide* by Mary Pope Osborne), television resources such as the Discovery Channel and Animal Planet, and so on.
- Relate the text directly to the topic of dolphins by telling students, "The text we will be reading gives lots of information about dolphins."
- While you are reading through the book with the students, continue to add to the B-K-W-L-Q chart.

Instructional Materials

- B-K-W-L-Q chart from *Tools for Teaching Content Literacy* by Janet Allen
- Comprehensible input about dolphins
- *Dolphins* by Victoria St. John
- Making-connections bookmarks

figure 5.4 *Viviana, Jose, and Daniel's making-connections bookmarks.*

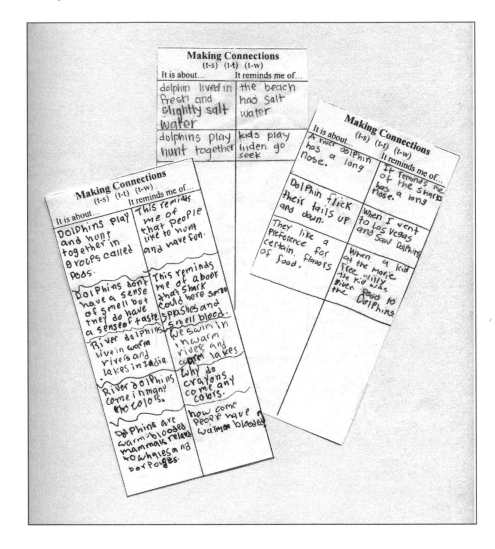

Give Information As you read a short section of the book *Dolphins*, encourage students to follow along. Think aloud as you read: "This reminds me of...." Then stop and record your connection on the making-connections bookmark. Be sure students understand what it was you were reading in the text that prompted your connection. Pay special attention to text-to-text connections.

Active Involvement Start with something such as, "Let's give this a try. Read the book with a partner, and as you are reading, think aloud about your connections. Then take some time to write down your connections and what the text was on your making-connections bookmark. Be sure to share your connections to the text with your partner." See figure 5.4, which shows a making-connection bookmark.

Off You Go "Now that you know how to use the making-connections bookmark to record your connections while you are reading informational text, we'll keep a pile of the bookmarks on the table. Feel free to use one to record your connections as you read. This is one way to use what you already know to understand the book."

2: Asking Questions

Teaching Moves

Start-up/Connection

Instructional Materials

- ☐ **Comprehensible input about Crazy Horse and the Lakota Nation**
- ☐ *Crazy Horse's Vision* **by Joseph Bruchac**
- ☐ **Anchor chart for "I wonder..." poem**
- ☐ **Strategy application notebooks**

- Ask a question to elicit students' prior knowledge about Crazy Horse and the Lakota.
- Have students share their experiences with Crazy Horse. (Our students have lots of experience with this topic because they study the Plains Indians through literature as well as a supplemental reading program that includes a video about Crazy Horse.) Include students' experiences and what they know through other means such as TV, movies, the Internet, and cultural connections.
- Provide comprehensible input about Crazy Horse and the Lakota, such as the video *Crazy Horse and the Lakota Sioux Indians* by Questar Inc., Web sites, other books (*The Life and Death of Crazy Horse* by Russell Freeman and *The Return of Crazy Horse* by William Kotzwinkle), television resources such as the Discovery Channel and the History Channel, and so on.
- Relate the text directly to the topic of Crazy Horse by telling students, "Today we're going to read a story about Crazy Horse when he was young. It's titled *Crazy Horse's Vision.*"

Give Information Before you read the book *Crazy Horse's Vision,* model your thinking about the book by recording some of your wonderings about the title, the table of contents, and the pictures in the book on an "I wonder..." anchor chart. Explain to students that asking questions and wondering about what they are reading helps them understand the text. Think aloud for your students about your wonderings as you write them. Then continue to model your wonderings and record them on the anchor chart in the form of a poem as you read through the text.

"I wonder..." Poem about Crazy Horse

I wonder why they called him Crazy Horse.
I wonder what it means to be brave if you are Lakota.
I wonder why the wild horse could not throw him.
I wonder what it feels like to kill a buffalo with a bow and arrow.

I wonder why the army came to keep peace between the white settlers and the Lakota.
I wonder why the army fired their rifles at the Lakota even though Chief Conquering Bear offered to pay a mule and five horses for the settler's cow that was killed.
I wonder why he thought he needed a vision to guide him even though he was still young.
I wonder why it took three days and nights before he had a vision.
I wonder how going to a sweathouse could help him prepare for a vision.
I wonder how Crazy Horse was able to "keep nothing for himself" like he was told in his vision.
I wonder why they called him Crazy Horse.

Active Involvement Read the book with a partner, and as you are reading think aloud about your wonderings. Then take some time to write down your wonderings on your 'I wonder...' pages in your strategy application notebook." Model this for students. "Be sure to share your wonderings about the text with your partner." See figures 5.5 and 5.6 for examples.

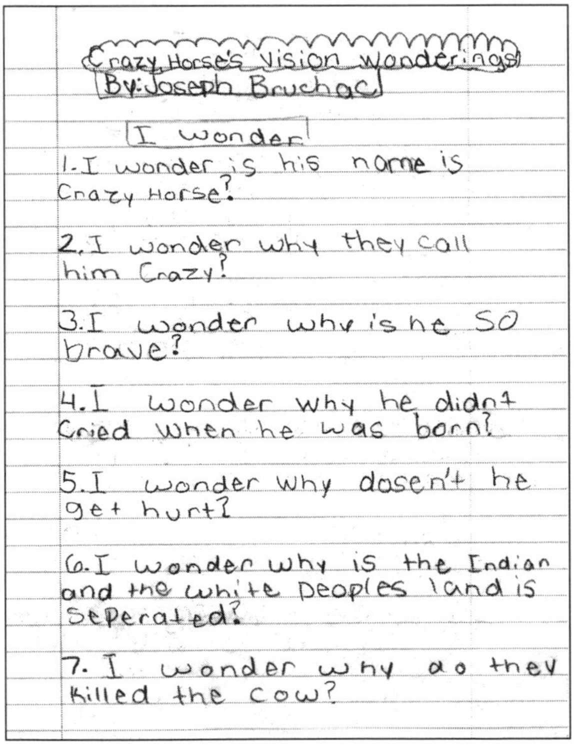

Crazy Horse's Vision Wonderings
By: Joseph Bruchac

I wonder

1. I wonder is his name is Crazy Horse?

2. I wonder why they call him Crazy?

3. I wonder why is he so brave?

4. I wonder why he didn't Cried when he was born?

5. I wonder why dosen't he get hurt?

6. I wonder why is the Indian and the white peoples land is seperated?

7. I wonder why do they killed the cow?

figure 5.5 *Juli modeled how to write a poem from her wonderings. Veronica was then able to make this list of what she wondered about to use for her poem.*

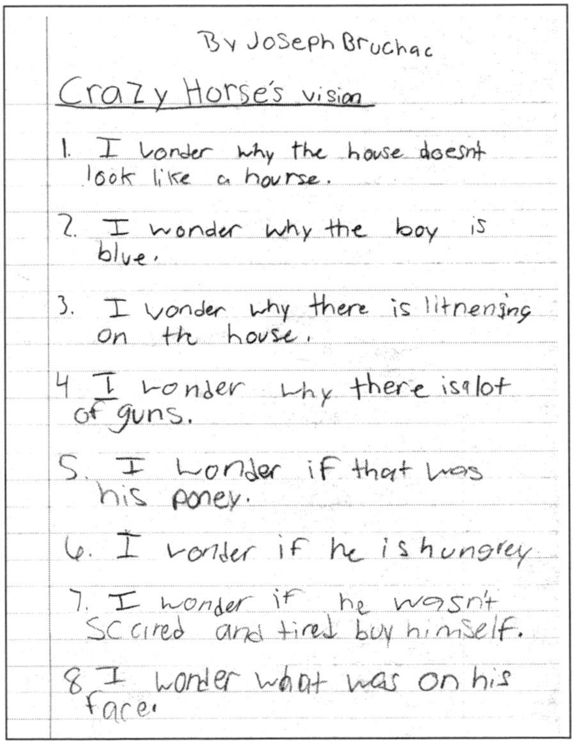

By Joseph Bruchac

Crazy Horse's vision

1. I wonder why the house doesn't look like a hourse.

2. I wonder why the boy is blue.

3. I wonder why there is litnening on the house.

4 I wonder why there is a lot of guns.

5. I wonder if that was his poney.

6. I wonder if he is hungrey

7. I wonder if he wasn't scared and tired buy himself.

8 I wonder what was on his face.

figure 5.6 *Patty wonders about* Crazy Horse's Vision *in her notebook.*

Off You Go When students are comfortable reading *Crazy Horse's Vision* with a partner and recording their wonderings in their strategy application notebook, give them the opportunity to work independently and create "I wonder. . ." poems (Tovani 2000, p. 83). To create "I wonder. . ." poems, model the activity first yourself. Show students how you take your questions and wonderings and rewrite them as poems. Then have students give it a try.

3: Visualizing — Creating Mental Images

Teaching Moves

Start-up/Connection

Instructional Materials
- Comprehensible input about the orchestra
- Sergei Prokofiev's *Peter and the Wolf* (with CD), illus. by Peter Malone, retold by Janet Schulman
- Strategy application notebooks

- Ask a question to elicit students' prior knowledge about orchestras.
- Have students share their experiences with orchestras. (Our students visit the orchestra for a performance each year, so they have experiences to share. Also, some of our parents are in orchestras that perform music from other cultures and countries.)
- Brainstorm a variety of characteristics for orchestras, such as the location, the instruments, the musicians, and the conductor. Include students' experiences and what they know through other means such as TV, movies, the Internet, and cultural connections.
- Provide comprehensible input about orchestras: field trips to hear an orchestra, and television shows of orchestra performances.
- Directly relate the text to the topic of orchestras by telling students, "Today we're going to listen to a recording of an orchestra performing *Peter and the Wolf* while we read the book."

Give Information Discuss with students how musical composers tell stories with their music. Sometimes they add words to the music and sometimes they don't. *Peter and the Wolf* has narrated text that tells the story as the musicians play. Listeners create mental images or movies in their minds of what they are hearing. This is one way of visualizing the story that the composer tells through the music.

Active Involvement Show students the pictures in the book as you play the music. Stop frequently to talk about the movies they are making in their minds. Encourage them to share their visualizations of the music, by modeling for them as you listen and sharing your own visualizations.

Off You Go When students are able to discuss their mental images of the recording of *Peter and the Wolf*, hand out their strategy applications notebooks so they may draw their mental images as they continue to listen, as in figures 5.7 and 5.8. To provide opportunities for using oral language, continue to stop from time to time and have students discuss with a partner what they are visualizing.

figure 5.7   *Johnny understood* Peter and the Wolf *as a problem between the duck and the wolf.*

figure 5.8   *A visualization based on* Peter and the Wolf.

Instructional Materials

- *Judge Rabbit and the Tree Spirit: A Folktale from Cambodia* **by Cathy Spagnoli and Lina Mao Wall** (available online from International Children's Digital Library as well as in traditional book format)
- **Folktales and legends from the International Children's Digital Library at the University of Maryland, http://www.icdlbooks.org/**
- **Two-column anchor chart labeled "Clues from the Text That Help Us Infer When We are Reading Folktales and Legends"**
- **Strategy application notebooks**

4: Inferring

Teaching Moves

Start-up/Connection To draw on prior knowledge, say to students, "Before we start reading *Judge Rabbit and the Tree Spirit: A Folktale from Cambodia,* let's talk about what we already know about folktales and legends." Have a conversation with the students about what folktales and legends they know and what they have learned from them. Students can briefly share folktales and legends from their own cultures.

Give Information Explain to students that folktales and legends come from many different cultures. Often they are not written down but are passed orally from generation to generation. They are used to teach lessons. In the Cambodian culture, folktales are very important because they teach traditional values. In the evenings in Cambodia, grandparents told them to their grandchildren. As you read aloud *Judge Rabbit and the Tree Spirit: A Folktale from Cambodia,* think aloud for the students as a model of how you use your prior knowledge, along with clues in the text, to help you draw conclusions from the folktale and infer the meaning. Think aloud about what values you infer from the folktale. As you read the folktale, jot down on the two-column chart what you infer and what the text said that caused you to infer.

Active Involvement While you are reading aloud, encourage students to discuss their connections to the folktale and how their prior knowledge and clues in the text help them draw conclusions. Add their inferences to the class chart.

Overhead Transparency We read *Judge Rabbit and the Tree Spirit: A Folktale from Cambodia*. We inferred from the text using our schema, the pictures, and the clues we found in the folktale.

Clues from the Text That Help Us Infer When We Are Reading *Judge Rabbit and the Tree Spirit: A Folktale from Cambodia*	
What the Folktale Said	**We Infer That**
The coconut trees seemed to shiver in fright.	Something bad is going to happen.
The heart-shaped leaves of the banyan tree seemed to rattle uneasily. Shadows danced along its roots.	There is something special about the banyan tree. It is not a regular tree.
Inside him, two minds and two hearts struggled.	The husband didn't know what to do. Should he go to war or should he go home to his wife?
Then the tree spirit, who could change his shape, made himself look just like her husband.	The spirit wants to make the wife happy because she is beautiful and she is crying.
"Who is who?" cried the wife. "Why do I see two of you?"	The wife is going to be very confused because she sees two husbands.
The unhappy husband told the rabbit his troubles. Judge Rabbit scratched his ear. "Don't worry," he said.	Judge Rabbit must be very smart because he tells the husband not to worry. He may have a plan to help the husband.

Off You Go Provide copies of other Judge Rabbit folktales for students to read with partners. Encourage them to talk about how their prior knowledge helps them infer meaning from the folktales. Have students use sticky notes to indicate the clues in the text that help them infer. Students use the two-column chart to record what the folktale says and what they infer in their strategy application notebooks. See Appendix for another Judge Rabbit folktale, "Judge Rabbit and the Snail Race."

5: Determining Importance in Nonfiction

Teaching Moves

Start-up/Connection

- Ask questions to elicit students' prior knowledge about deserts, and ask them if they have heard of the Sonoran Desert.
- Have students share their experiences with deserts.
- Brainstorm a variety of characteristics for deserts. Include students' experiences and what they know through other means such as TV, movies, the Internet, and cultural connections.
- Provide comprehensible input about the Sonoran Desert, such as

---

Instructional Materials

- ☐ **Comprehensible input about the Sonoran Desert**
- ☐ ***A Desert Scrapbook: Dawn to Dusk in the Sonoran Desert* by Virginia Wright-Frierson**
- ☐ **Overhead transparency for FQR form**

the Web site for the Arizona–Sonora Desert Museum, http://www
.desertmuseum.org/, other books (*Cactus Hotel* by Brenda Z. Guiberson
and *Correctamundo: Prickly Pete's Guide to Desert Facts & Cactifracts*
by David Lazaroff), television resources such as the Discovery
Channel, National Geographic Channel, and so on.

- Relate the text directly to the topic of the Sonoran Desert by telling
  students, "We're going to read a book about an artist who lives in the
  Sonoran Desert and keeps a notebook about what she notices—all the
  things she sees."

Give Information Before reading aloud *A Desert Scrapbook: Dawn to Dusk in
the Sonoran Desert,* explain the three-column FQR form you will use to
record facts you learn, questions you have, and your responses as you read.
Take a picture walk through the book. Point out the labels the author added
to the book as well as the photographs and notebook pages. Talk about how
the author added information to the pages of the book.

Active Involvement Read through the book slowly, stopping frequently to talk
with the students about what they are learning about the Sonoran Desert and
what to add to the FQR form. As you read, draw students into a conversation
about why this book is called a scrapbook. Help them understand that a
scrapbook is usually a blank book where you can paste in photos, do
drawings and paintings, write captions and labels, and so on. Stop frequently
and let them talk to a partner about the nonfiction conventions (such as
drawings, labels, and captions) they notice in the book and how they help
them learn new information.

Overhead Transparency for FQR Form

A Desert Scrapbook: Dawn to Dusk in the Sonoran Desert by Virginia Wright-Frierson		
Facts	**Questions**	**Response**
Animals are active in the cool, early morning.	How come they come out only during the early morning or late at night?	Maybe it's because at night they like to hunt and during the day they like to sleep.
Vultures eat only dead stuff.	Why did the artist wave her arms to show she wasn't dead?	She waved her arms because she didn't want to get eaten.
The roadrunner eats Zebra Tailed lizards.	Why do they call it a Zebra Tailed lizard?	Maybe because the tail has black and white stripes.
The cactus wren builds her nest in the Jumping Cholla cactus.	Why does the bird go back to get the beetle larvae?	She wants to feed them to the babies because they look like worms, and birds eat worms.
	Why doesn't the cactus poke the bird?	Because the bird has cactus-proof feathers.

Off You Go Give each student an FQR form for his or her strategy application notebook. This form is a scaffold to help students understand how to determine what is important in the text they are reading. Allow students to read other books about the Sonoran Desert or other topics, based on their interests, as they fill out their FQR forms. In addition, provide a supply of FQR forms for students to use when they read nonfiction or informational text.

6: Synthesizing

Teaching Moves

Start-up/Connection Before reading aloud the story *Bread Song,* have a conversation with the students about what they know about Thailand. Provide background information if necessary. Have students look at the illustrations in the book and talk about what they notice. Encourage discussion about the contrasts between the old New England seaport where the story takes place and Thailand, the home of the boy's family.

Give Information Explain to students that as you read aloud *Bread Song,* you will be synthesizing. That means you will keep track of how your thinking changes as you are reading. Use the synthesizing frame to help students understand how your thinking changes as you read. Display the synthesizing frame on the overhead projector.

Synthesizing Frame

Before we started reading *Bread Song,* I was thinking that ____.
Then when we first started reading, I thought it was going to be about ____ because ____.
But then we read something different about ____.
So I'm changing my thinking because ____.

Active Involvement To model synthesizing, read the story aloud and think aloud about how your thinking is changing as you read. Use sticky notes to mark the places in the text where your thinking changes. Stop frequently to ask students where their thinking is changing. Have them read aloud the places in the text where their thinking changed and explain how it changed. Write your synthesizing on the overhead transparency as a model for students.

Off You Go After reading the story aloud, students can place their sticky notes in their strategy application notebooks and use the synthesizing frame to record their thinking. Students can also use the synthesizing frame to record their thinking when they read other texts.

Students' Synthesizing Frames *for* Bread Song

Before I started reading, I was thinking that the text was about bread because the title is *Bread Song.*

Then when we first started reading, I still thought it was going to be about bread because the boy and his grandfather went to a bakery.

But then we read something different about how bread sings and how the boy loves his grandfather.

So I'm changing my thinking because at the end of the story the boy learns English.

Before I started reading, I was thinking the text was about bread because there is bread on the cover and the title is *Bread Song*.

Then when we started reading, I thought it was going to be about change.

But then we read something different about eating a roll and hearing the bread sing.

So I'm changing my thinking because the boy speaks English at the end.

Books for Teaching Strategies to Younger English Language Learners

Intermediate Stage

Making Connections

A Is for Asia by Cynthia Chin-Lee
Dolphins by Victoria St. John
Dumpling Soup by Jama Kim Rattigan
First Day in Grapes by L. King Perez
La Mariposa by Francisco Jimenez

Asking Questions

1,000 Questions and Answers by Robin Kerrod
A Boy Called Slow: The True Story of Sitting Bull by Joseph Bruchac
Crazy Horse's Vision by Joseph Bruchac
Why I Sneeze, Shiver, Hiccup, & Yawn (Let's-Read-and-Find-Out Science 2 series) by Melvin Berger
Why?: The Best Ever Question and Answer Book About Nature, Science and the World Around You by Catherine Ripley

Visualizing

From the Belly Button of the Moon and Other Summer Poems by Francisco X. Alarcon
I'm in Charge of Celebrations by Byrd Baylor
Iguanas in the Snow and Other Winter Poems by Francisco X. Alarcon
Sagawa, The Chinese Siamese Cat by Amy Tan
Sergei Prokofiev's *Peter and the Wolf* (with CD), illust. by Peter Malone, retold by Janet Schulman

Inferring

Fables by Arnold Lobel
Juan Bobo Goes to Work: A Puerto Rican Folktale by Marisa Montes
Judge Rabbit and the Tree Spirit, A Folktale from Cambodia by Cathy
  Spagnoli and Lina Mao Wall
Roadrunner's Dance by Rodolfo Anaya
Sitti's Secrets by Naomi Shihab Nye

Determining Importance in Nonfiction

A Desert Scrapbook: Dawn to Dusk in the Sonoran Desert by Virginia
  Wright-Frierson
A North American Rain Forest Scrapbook by Virginia Wright-Frierson
An Island Scrapbook: Dawn to Dusk on a Barrier Island by Virginia
  Wright-Frierson
Cactus Hotel by Brenda Z. Guiberson
Everglades by Jean Craighead George
Correctamundo: Prickly Pete's Guide to Desert Facts & Cactifracts by
  David Lazaroff

Synthesizing

Baseball Saved Us by Ken Mochizuki
Bread Song by Frederick Lipp
The Bracelet by Yoshiko Uchida
Chato's Kitchen by Gary Soto

Older English Language Learners in Real Time

"What's going on in this story?" the sixth-grade English Language Learner asked. The boy looked puzzled. "I'm so confused. It keeps changing back and forth."

As kids move into higher stages, texts become more complex. "The Dog of Pompeii," a short story by Louis Untermeyer from the sixth-grade literature anthology, includes flashbacks. It tells the story of Tito, a blind orphan, and his dog, who experience the eruption of Vesuvius. The kids often find it very confusing.

This short story uses complex literary devices such as flashbacks and fore-shadowing that relate to the author's development of time and sequence. Kids need to figure out the time sequence in this short story because it is critical to understanding the content.

To help students learn to determine importance in text and sequence events in the short story, Juli used the book *The Secrets of Vesuvius* by Sara C. Bisal. She did this to help the students get a clear sense of the eruption of Vesuvius and the ensuing events. She also read aloud sections from *Volcano* by Patricia Lauber and *Pompeii: The Vanished City* by Time-Life Books. These books provided the necessary comprehensible input for students to understand the short story.

Because the events in the short story were out of order, she decided to provide a time line to help students sequence the different scenes. At the left end of the time line, she wrote, "Vesuvius Erupts," and on the right end, she wrote, "Pompeii Ruins Discovered." Then students chose events from the story, wrote a sentence or two on a sticky note to describe the events, and placed their sticky notes on the time line.

There was lots of negotiation between the students about the order of the sticky notes. "I think this came first," one student would say, and another would answer, "Look at the story. You can tell the author is flashing back because...." By using the time line and providing comprehensible input about the eruption of Vesuvius, students were able to determine importance in the text. Once they ordered the events of the story, they could easily discuss the difference between fact and opinion as it related to the ruins of Pompeii.

In the end, it all worked out. "I get it now," the first student commented. "I just needed to know when everything happened."

Lesson Plans for Older English Language Learners

1: Making Connections

Teaching Moves

Start-up/Connection

- Ask a question to elicit students' prior knowledge about wolves and dogs.
- Have students share their experiences with wolves and dogs.
- Brainstorm a variety of characteristics for wolves and dogs, such as habitat, food, and family life. Include students' experiences and what they know through other means such as TV, movies, the Internet, and cultural connections.
- Provide comprehensible input about wolves, such as the video *Wolves: A Legend Returns to Yellowstone* by National Geographic, Web sites, other books (*Wolves* by Gail Gibbons, *Walk with a Wolf* by Janni Howker, and *Wolves* by Seymour Simon), and television resources such as the Discovery Channel, Animal Planet, and the National Geographic Channel.
- With students' input, draw a graphic organizer such as a Venn diagram to categorize what they contribute about the similarities and differences between dogs and wolves.
- Relate the text directly to the topic of dogs and wolves by telling students, "Today we are going to read about wolves and how dogs evolved from wolves."

- Compare what students learn as they read the article "Wolf to Woof: Evolution of Dogs" and other texts to the Venn diagram they developed.

Give Information As you read aloud a short section of the magazine article "Wolf to Woof" (*Look to the North: A Wolf Pup Diary* by Jean Craighead George may be substituted for the magazine article), think aloud as you read. Say, "This reminds me of...." Then stop and record the words in the article and your connection to another text on the overhead transparency. Be sure students understand what you were reading in the text that prompted your connection. Pay special attention to text-to-text connections. Explain how the connection you make helps you understand what you are reading.

Active Involvement "Finish reading the magazine article with a partner, and think aloud about your connections as you read. Then take some time to write the words in the text and your connection to another text on a two-column chart in your strategy application notebook. Be sure to include the title of the texts for your connections. Be sure to share your connections to the text with your partner and let him or her know how your connections help you understand the book."

Overhead Transparency

Making Text-to-Text Connections for "From Wolf to Woof: Evolution of Dogs" and *Wolves*	
Words in the Text—"From Wolf to Woof: Evolution of Dogs"	**My Connection to *Wolves* by Gail Gibbons**
"About 800,000 years ago wolves crossed to Arctic North America."	It reminds us of how the first ancestor of wolves lived more than 50 million years ago.
"Early canids reached Europe seven million years ago, but it was Eucyon moving west six to four million years ago, that gave rise to most modern canids, including wolves, coyotes, and jackals."	It reminds us of what the book said, that wolves are members of the dog family called Canidae and that all dogs are related to wolves.
"Range of the grey wolf 100,000 years ago" (from the map Canid Migrations).	It reminds us of how wolves used to live all around the world and how people hunted them and took over much of their territory. According to the book *Wolves,* they are in danger of extinction.

Off You Go "Now that you know how to use the two-column chart to record your text-to-text connections while you read nonfiction text, remember to keep track of your connections while you read other nonfiction text. Feel free to use your strategy application notebooks for a two-column chart to record your connections as you read."

Instructional Materials

- **Comprehensible input about the Underground Railroad**
- **...*If You Traveled on The Underground Railroad* by Ellen Levine**
- **"I wonder..." anchor chart**
- **Strategy application notebooks**
- **"I wonder..." poems**

2: Asking Questions

Teaching Moves

Before starting this lesson, it is a good idea to clarify the meaning of the term *Underground Railroad* with the students. To do this we read aloud the book *Follow the Drinking Gourd* by Jeanette Winter. A note at the beginning of the story explains the Underground Railroad. Outey thinks this is important so that students are not confused. "When I first came to the United States, it took me a while to understand that the Underground Railroad wasn't really under the ground and that there wasn't any railroad," she says. "I had to learn that the meaning of *underground* in this context was 'done in secret' or 'undercover.' In addition, over time, I realized that the word *railroad* referred to a way of transporting people and not an actual railroad."

A friend living in the United States but originally from England put it this way: "To me, *Underground Railroad* has always been a very confusing term. The first thing that comes to mind when I hear it is the London Underground, the Tube. I picture an American asking the way to the nearest Tube station! But you must admit, the fact it was neither underground nor a railroad is pretty confusing."

Start-up/Connection

- Ask a question to elicit students' prior knowledge about the Underground Railroad.
- Have students share their experiences with the topic. Students from other countries may have experiences to share about other ways people have escaped.
- Brainstorm a variety of characteristics for the Underground Railroad, such as where it was, how people found it, how they traveled on it, and where they were going. Include students' experiences and what they know through other means such as TV, movies, the Internet, and cultural connections.
- With students' input, draw a graphic organizer such as a B-K-W-L-Q chart from Janet Allen's *Tools for Teaching Content Literacy* to put students' contributions in categories.
- Provide comprehensible input about the topic: a Web site simulation of the Underground Railroad at http://www.nationalgeographic.com/railroad/, other books (*Aunt Harriet's Underground Railroad in the Sky* by Faith Ringgold, *Follow the Drinking Gourd* by Jeanette Winter, *Sweet Clara and the Freedom Quilt* by Deborah Hopkinson), television resources such as the Discovery Channel, the History Channel, the National Geographic Channel, and so forth.
- Directly relate the text ...*If You Traveled on The Underground Railroad* by Ellen Levine to the topic of the Underground Railroad by telling students, "The book we will be reading is about the Underground Railroad and how slaves escaped to freedom."
- While you are reading through the book with the students, continue to add to the B-K-W-L-Q chart.

Give Information Before you read . . . *If You Traveled on The Underground Railroad,* model your thinking by recording some of your wonderings about the title, the table of contents, and the pictures from the book on an "I wonder . . ." anchor chart. Explain to students that asking questions and wondering about what they are reading helps them understand the text. Think aloud for your students about your wonderings as you write them on the chart. Point out to students that the table of contents is organized around a series of questions that are answered in the text. Then continue to model your wonderings and record them on the anchor chart as you read through the text.

Active Involvement "Read the book with a partner and think aloud about your wonderings as you read. Then take some time to write down your wonderings on your 'I wonder . . .' pages in your strategy application notebook." (Model this for students.) "Be sure to share your wonderings about the text with your partner." See the examples in figures 5.9 and 5.10.

Off You Go When students are comfortable reading . . . *If You Traveled on The Underground Railroad* with a partner and recording their wonderings in their strategy application notebooks, give them the opportunity to work independently and create "I wonder . . ." poems. To create the poems, first model the activity yourself. Show students how you take your questions and wonderings and rewrite them as poems. Then have students try it.

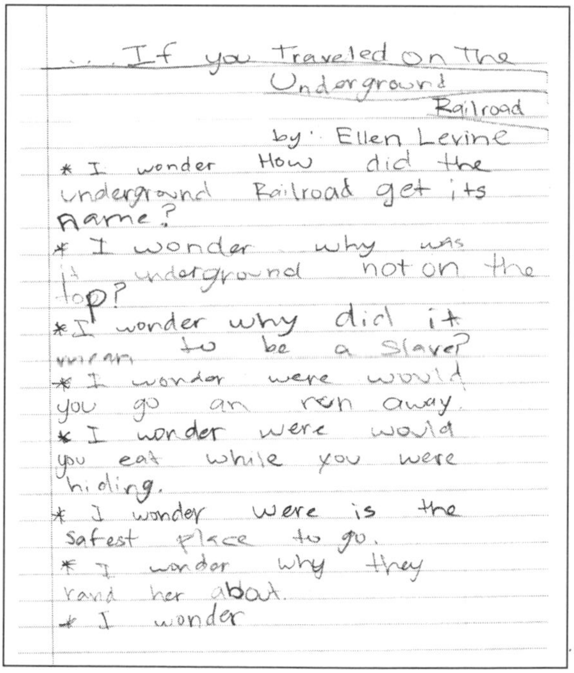

...If you Traveled on The Underground Railroad
by: Ellen Levine
* I wonder How did the underground Railroad get its name?
* I wonder why was it underground not on the top?
* I wonder why did it mean to be a Slave?
* I wonder were would you go an run away.
* I wonder were would you eat while you were hiding.
* I wonder were is the safest place to go.
* I wonder why they rand her about.
* I wonder

figure 5.9 *Mary makes a list of her wonderings.*

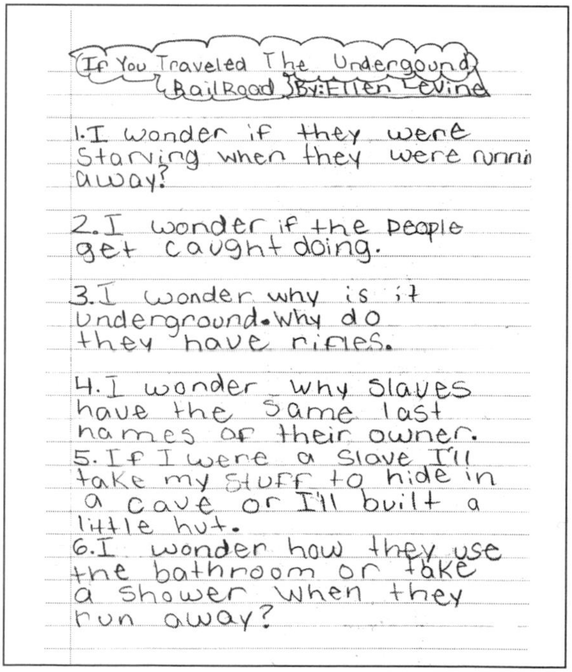

If You Traveled The Undergound RailRoad By: Ellen Levine
1. I wonder if they were Starving when they were runnin away?
2. I wonder if the people get caught doing.
3. I wonder why is it Underground. Why do they have rifles.
4. I wonder why slaves have the same last names of their owner.
5. If I were a slave I'll take my stuff to hide in a cave or I'll built a little hut.
6. I wonder how they use the bathroom or take a shower when they run away?

figure 5.10 *Veronica records her thinking on an "I wonder . . ." page.*

Instructional Materials

- Comprehensible input about museums
- Saint Saens's *Carnival of the Animals* (with CD) by John Lithgow
- Strategy application notebooks

3: Visualizing—Creating Mental Images

Teaching Moves

Start-up/Connection Ask students to think about the last time they went on a school field trip. Discuss where they went and what they did. Find out if the students have ever visited a museum. If not, provide comprehensible input from museum Web sites.

Give Information Discuss with students how musical composers tell stories with their music. Sometimes they add words to the music and sometimes they turn their words and music into operas. *Carnival of the Animals* was turned into an opera in New York City in 2003. Show students the picture of the New York City Ballet in costume at the end of the book. Explain that what listeners do as they listen to the music is create mental images or movies in their minds of what they are hearing. This is one way of visualizing the story that the composer tells through the music.

Active Involvement Show the pictures in the book to the students while you play the music. As they listen, stop frequently to talk about the movies they are making in their minds. Encourage them to share their visualizations of the music, sharing your own visualizations as models. Samples of student visualizations are in figures 5.11 and 5.12.

Off You Go When students are able to discuss their mental images of the recording of *Carnival of the Animals,* hand out their strategy application

figure 5.11 *Casey visualizes in a variety of ways.*

figure 5.12 *Gladys finds many ways to represent her mental images of* Carnival of the Animals *in her strategy application notebook.*

notebooks so they can draw their mental images as they continue to listen. To provide opportunities for using oral language, continue to stop from time to time and have students share with a partner about what they are visualizing.

4: Inferring

Teaching Moves

Start-up/Connection: To draw on prior knowledge, say to students, "Before we start reading *Prietita and The Ghost Woman,* let's talk about what we know about folktales and legends." Have a conversation with the students about what folktales and legends they know and what they have learned from them. List the folktales and legends that students mention on a chart.

Give Information: Explain to students that folktales and legends come from many different cultures. Often they are not written down but passed from generation to generation by word of mouth. The legend of La Llorona has many different retellings and versions. As you read aloud *Prietita and The Ghost Woman,* think aloud for the students to model how you use your prior knowledge and clues in the text to help you draw conclusions from the legend and infer the meaning.

Active Involvement: While you are reading, encourage students to discuss their connections to the legend and how their prior knowledge and clues in the text help them draw conclusions from the folktale. Have them add their inferences to the T-chart using sticky notes to keep track of the clues from the text.

Inferring from Folktales: *Prietita and the Ghost Woman* by Gloria Anzaldua	
What the Folktale Says	**What I Infer**
She knows lots of remedies.	La curandera knows a lot about medicine that doesn't come from the store.
"Prietita, Mami feels very bad. It's the old sickness again," said Miranda.	Mami might have been sick a lot before.
"It's very dangerous to go there. I've heard that they shoot trespassers," said la curandera.	They don't want people coming there without permission.
She thought she heard a crying sound and she remembered her grandmother's stories of La Llorona.	Prietita shivered because she was scared of La Llorona. She thought that she stole children.
The Ghost Woman floated above the lagoon. Prietita followed her. Soon the woman stopped and pointed to a spot on the ground.	Prietita stopped being afraid because the Ghost Woman helped her find the leaves from the rue plant that she was looking for.
"Perhaps she is not what others think she is," said Doña Lola.	Sometimes you can be wrong even if you think you know something. You can be scared because of what someone told you about the Ghost Woman.

Instructional Materials

- *Prietita and The Ghost Woman* by Gloria Anzaldua
- Strategy application notebooks
- Folktales and legends from the International Children's Digital Library at the University of Maryland, http://www.icdlbooks.org/
- Overhead transparency for two-column chart labeled "Clues from the Text That Help Us Infer When We Are Reading Folktales and Legends"
- Strategy application notebooks

Off You Go Provide additional copies of other versions of the La Llorona legend for students to read with partners such as *La Llorona, The Weeping Woman* by Joe Hayes. Encourage them to talk about how they infer meaning from the different versions of the legends. Have students use sticky notes to indicate the clues in the text that help them infer. Students can also be encouraged to use two-column charts to record what the folktale says and what they infer in their strategy application notebooks.

5: Determining Importance in Nonfiction

Teaching Moves

Start-up/Connection

- Ask a question to elicit students' prior knowledge about informational text.
- Have students share and talk about informational texts they have read.
- Brainstorm a variety of characteristics for informational text, such as text features and factual information. Include students' experiences and what they know through other means such as TV, movies, the Internet, and cultural connections.
- Directly relate the text *Do Tarantulas Have Teeth? Questions and Answers About Poisonous Creatures* by Melvin and Gilda Berger to the topic of informational text by telling students, "The book we will be reading is filled with facts and information about poisonous creatures. The first animal it discusses is the tarantula."

Give Information Explain to students that you will be using the FQR form to write the important facts you learn about tarantulas and other poisonous animals as you read the book. Model how to use the form by thinking aloud as you fill it in.

FQR Form for *Do Tarantulas Have Teeth? Questions and Answers About Poisonous Creatures* by Melvin and Gilda Berger		
Facts	**Questions**	**Response**
After poisonous animals use up their venom, they make more.	How do the poisonous animals produce venom?	We thought that bees died after they used their venom. Now we wonder if they make new venom instead of dying.
Tarantulas have very sharp teeth called fangs for catching and killing their prey.	We wonder if when the tarantula loses its teeth, they grow back. How do they grow new teeth?	We never heard about a tarantula losing a tooth.
Tarantulas cannot chew. They can only drink and soak up liquids.	How does the food dissolve in their bodies?	We think they may eat like when we eat a Slurpee.

Active Involvement As you read the book with the group, students can add information to the FQR form when they find important facts in the text.

Off You Go After you finish reading several pages in the book, hand out copies of the book. Provide one for each student in the group. Give students an FQR form that they can add to their strategy application notebooks. Have students locate facts from their books about other poisonous animals such as the black widow spider and the rattlesnake and fill in the form as they read. Encourage them to share their facts, questions, and responses with a partner.

6: Synthesizing

Teaching Moves

Instructional Materials
- *Love as Strong as Ginger* by Lenore Look
- Sticky notes
- Strategy application notebooks
- Overhead transparency for synthesizing frame

Start-up/Connection Before reading aloud *Love as Strong as Ginger,* have students use the title and the front cover illustration to predict what they think the story will be about. Provide pieces of ginger candy so they can taste ginger. Discuss what the title might mean.

Give Information Explain to students that they will be reading a story about a girl from China and her grandmother. They will use the synthesizing frame to help them understand how their thinking changes as they read.

> ### Synthesizing Frame
>
> Before we started reading *Love as Strong as Ginger*, I was thinking that
> ____.
> Then when we first started reading, I thought it was going to be about
> ____ because ____.
> But then we read something different about ____.
> So I'm changing my thinking because ____.

Active Involvement To model synthesizing, read the story aloud and think aloud about how your thinking is changing as you read. To model synthesizing, use the synthesizing frame and write your synthesizing on the overhead transparency. Encourage students to share their own synthesizing. As you read, stop frequently and have students use their strategy application notebooks to record their synthesizing. They can use the synthesizing frame as a way to scaffold their thinking. Have students read the places in the text where their thinking changed. Also have them talk to each other and explain how their thinking changed as they read.

> ### Rosa's Synthesizing Frame for Love as Strong as Ginger
>
> Before I started reading, I looked at the cover and the title and I was thinking that they were going to eat candy ginger.
> Then when we first started reading, I was thinking that it was going to be about crab because the only job the grandma can get is with crab.

But then we read something different about how the girl was going to say, "No!"

So I'm changing my thinking because the girl is going to teach her grandma how to speak English so she can get a better job.

Oscar's Synthesizing Frame for Love as Strong as Ginger

Before I started reading, I was thinking that the text was about food because of the cover and the title about ginger.

Then when we first started reading, I thought it was going to be about teaching how to make food because the grandma was cooking.

But then we read something different about how the little girl is saying that she wants to be like her grandma.

So I'm changing my thinking because I think the story was about cracking crabs.

Off You Go Allow students to use the synthesizing frame as they read additional selections. Have them read along with a partner to talk about their synthesizing and indicate the places in their reading where their thinking changes. Students can also use the synthesizing frame to add their synthesizing to their strategy application notebooks.

Texts for Teaching Strategies to Older English Language Learners

Intermediate Stage

Making Connections

"Wolf to Woof: Evolution of Dogs" from *National Geographic* magazine January 2002
Look to the North: A Wolf Pup Diary by Jean Craighead George
My Very Own Room by Amada Irma Perez
My Name Was Hussein by Hristo Kyuchukov
Smoky Night by Eve Bunting
Wolves by Gail Gibbons

Asking Questions

Aunt Harriet's Underground Railroad in the Sky by Faith Ringgold
Follow the Drinking Gourd by Jeanette Winter
. . . If You Traveled on the Underground Railroad by Ellen Levine
Martin's Big Words by Doreen Rappaport
Sweet Clara and the Freedom Quilt by Deborah Hopkinson

Visualizing

Angels Ride Bikes and Other Fall Poems by Francisco X. Alarcon
Into the Sea by Brenda Z. Guiberson

Laughing Tomatoes and Other Spring Poems by Francisco X. Alarcon
Saint Saens's *Carnival of the Animals* (with CD) by John Lithgow
Wings by Christopher Myers

Inferring

Chato and the Party Animals by Gary Soto
The Green Frogs: A Korean Folktale by Yumi Heo
The Old Man and His Door by Gary Soto
La Llorona, The Weeping Woman by Joe Hayes
Prietita and the Ghost Woman by Gloria Anzaldua

Determining Importance in Nonfiction

Animal Defenses: How Animals Protect Themselves by Etta Kaner
Animals Nobody Loves by Seymour Simon
*Do Tarantulas Have Teeth? Questions and Answers About Poisonous
  Creatures* by Melvin and Gilda Berger
Exploding Ants: Amazing Facts About How Animals Adapt by
  Joanne Settel

Synthesizing

Angel Child, Dragon Child by Michele Surat
The Table Where Rich People Sit by Byrd Baylor
Love as Strong as Ginger by Lenore Look

ADVANCED

Younger English Language Learners in Real Time

Juli sat down at a table to interview students about synthesizing. It was toward the end of a unit of study about inquiry and investigation, and kids were finishing up their projects. They had chosen questions to investigate and then worked independently or in small groups to do research and prepare presentations on what they had learned.

To scaffold their use of the synthesizing strategy and to help them understand how their thinking changed, students used a synthesizing frame.

I first thought this...
But then I learned...
Next I learned...
But this changed everything because...
This is way different from what I thought at the beginning. My thinking changed because...

Jonathan was the first student to explain his thinking. "My question: Is there other life in the universe? I first thought this: that there was other life in the

figure 6.1 *(above left) Sammoon's chart presents the results of her research about the question, What is the solar system made of?*

figure 6.2 *(above center) Saroung Yoeun, a paraprofessional, reflects with Sokuntheer, Michelle, and Jeannie on ways that group work helps them use strategies.*

figure 6.3 *(above right) Viviana writes questions about her project.*

101

universe like different human beings like aliens and UFOs. But then I learned it takes a long time to send a message to another planet. Next I learned that people on Earth send a message by a gold disk. But this changed everything, because now I know that the people who send messages to different planets are waiting for an answer. This is way different from what I thought at the beginning. My thinking changed because now I know that if someone answers back, it means there is other life in the universe."

Daniel, eager to explain his thinking, was next. "I was investigating, What is air pressure? I first thought this: that air pressure was like a big cloud. But then I learned that air pressure is affected by two things: how much atmosphere there is and the mass of the planet, which determines the gravity that pulls the air down. But this changed everything! I erased the idea of the cloud in my head and put in the new idea. This is way different from what I thought at the beginning. My thinking changed because first I thought air pressure was a big cloud, and now I think air pressure is like a big wind that is affected by the atmosphere we have and how big is the planet and strong is the gravity."

figure 6.4 *When she investigates a question independently, Loren writes her synthesis on the synthesizing pyramid.*

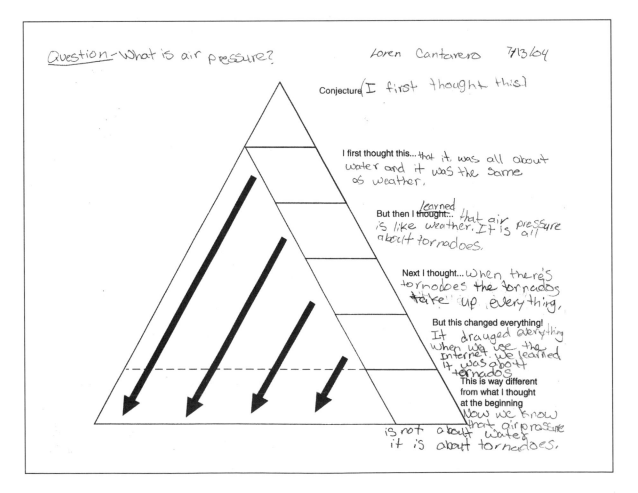

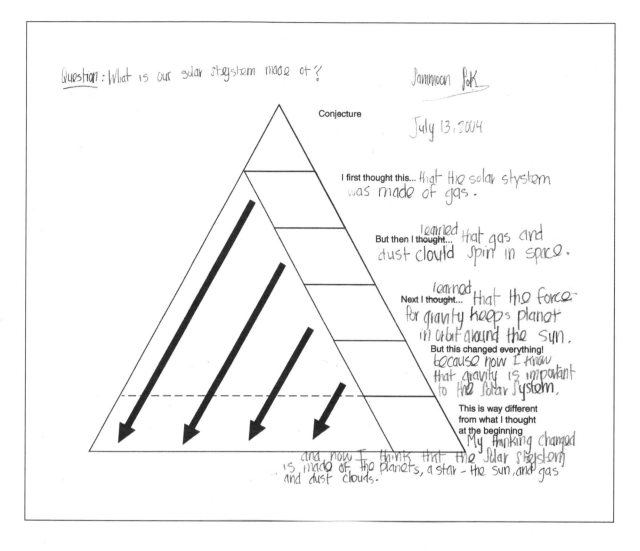

Question: What is our solar stsystem made ot?

Sammoon PoK

July 13, 2004

Conjecture

I first thought this... that the solar stystem was made of gas.

But then I thought... learned that gas and dust clould spin in space.

Next I thought... learned that the force for gravity keeps planet in orbit around the sun.

But this changed everything! because now I know that gravity is important to the solar system.

This is way different from what I thought at the beginning

My thinking changed and now I think that the solar stystem is made of the planets, a star - the sun, and gas and dust clouds.

Jeannie was the one who discovered, while she was synthesizing, that her question had changed. This discovery led to a revision of her original question for investigation and fed into the ultimate goal of the inquiry projects: to continue to ask questions that lead to more learning. "At first, my question was, What is the life cycle of a star? I first thought this: that stars have their own gravity and that stars are really hot. But then I learned that stars are like the sun. My question changed to 'What is a star?' Next I learned that if you have no sun the whole earth will be dark. But this changed everything, because now I thought about how stars are really important. This is way different from what I thought at the beginning. My thinking changed because now I know that stars bring us light and heat." Synthesizing helped her realize what she had learned during her inquiry and how her thinking changed. See figures 6.4 and 6.5 for two examples of how the synthesizing frame was used.

figure 6.5 *Sammoon synthesizes for her science inquiry project. She asks herself, "How has my thinking changed?"*

Lesson Plans for Younger English Language Learners

Instructional Materials

- *Dia's Story Cloth: The Hmong People's Journey of Freedom* by Dia Cha
- Sticky notes
- Overhead transparency for chart labeled "How well do I know these words?" from *Words, Words, Words* by Janet Allen, page 127
- Overhead transparency for two-column chart labeled "Connections/How It Helps Us Understand the Story"
- Strategy application notebooks

1: Making Connections

Teaching Moves

Start-up/Connection

BUILDING BACKGROUND

- Ask a question to elicit students' prior knowledge about the Hmong people of Laos.
- Have students share their experiences with the Hmong. We have a number of Hmong students at our school as well as a cultural program that brings a Hmong speaker to our school. The speaker discusses Hmong culture, such as art, music, dancing, way of life, clothing, and storytelling. Students also participate in making their own story cloth.
- Brainstorm what students know about the Hmong culture. Include students' experiences and what they know through other means such as TV, movies, the Internet, and cultural connections.
- If necessary, provide comprehensible input about the Hmong: Internet Web sites, other books (*The Whispering Cloth: A Refugee's Story* by Peggy Deitz Shea), and television resources such as the Discovery Channel, the History Channel, and National Geographic Channel.
- Relate the text directly to the topic of the Hmong by telling students, "The Hmong created story cloths as a way to tell their stories and record their history. The book we will read tells about how a story cloth was created."

DEVELOPING VOCABULARY

The importance of developing academic vocabulary for students at the advanced stage cannot be overemphasized. Many English Language Learners speak fluent English yet struggle to master content-area material. Janet Allen's *Words, Words, Words* (1999) provides extensive information about how to help students develop vocabulary and organize what they are learning. The book helps teachers incorporate vocabulary development in context.

Start by giving a copy of *Dia's Story Cloth* to each student in a small group. Ask students to look through the story and identify words and concepts that they need to have clarified. Chart their contributions on the overhead transparency for "How well do I know these words?" Write the word/concept as well as the sentence in which it is found.

Overhead Transparency

Words and Concepts We Want to Clarify

Ancestors: "A long time ago, my ancestors lived in China."
Fled: "... and fled across the river."
Tropical highlands: "They settled in the tropical highlands where no one had lived before."

Tended: "Both men and women tended the crops."
Thatched: "...a wood and bamboo house with a thatched roof made of palm leaves."
Warfare: "Laos was caught in warfare."

How Well Do I Know These Words and Concepts?			
Don't know at all	**Have seen or heard—don't know meaning**	**I think I know the meaning**	**I know a meaning**
tropical highlands	fled tended thatched	ancestors	warfare

Discuss the words and concepts to be clarified, providing definitions as needed.

Give Information Tell students that readers need to be able to explain how their connections help them understand what they are reading. Do shared reading with the story *Dia's Story Cloth*. Think aloud as you go, "This reminds me of..." and "That helps me understand this selection better because...." Read and think aloud for five to ten minutes.

Active Involvement "Everyone gets to try this out. Working together here at the table, we'll keep reading. We'll talk about how we activate our prior knowledge and how that helps us understand what we are reading. You can make your own connections while we are reading and share them with the group. Remember to let us know where you make the connection in the text and how making the connection helps you understand the story."

Overhead Transparency

Making-Connections for *Dia's Story Cloth*	
Connections	**How It Helps Us Understand the Story**
The pictures in the book remind us of last year when we had Hmong art.	Because Mrs. Lee came every week so we could learn about how they made the art and the Hmong culture.
The story cloth in the book reminds us of Mrs. Lee.	Because Mrs. Lee brought Hmong art and we cut out paper to make a story cloth. We did elephant footprints and snails, too.
The story cloth in the book reminds us of the story she told us.	Because bad guys were shooting at the people and they escaped just like on the story cloth.
The picture of the author, Dia Cha, at the back of the book, reminds us of the Hmong dancing.	Because on the last day of Hmong art we went to the cafeteria to watch the Hmong dances. They were dressed just like Dia Cha in the picture.

Off You Go "Now you are ready to work on the next section of the story. You'll work with your partner. First, look through the section and find the words and concepts you need to have clarified. Remember to write both the words you need to have clarified and the sentences where you found them in your strategy application notebook. Then spend some time talking about what the words mean. You may need to look up the definitions. Next, read through the text selection together by thinking aloud about the connections you are making. Think about how they help you understand the text better. Record your connections in your strategy application notebook. Use the two-column chart we made together as a model."

Instructional Materials

- Copies of history textbook *A New Nation, Adventures in Time and Place* by McGraw Hill, "Columbus and the Taino"
- Overhead transparency for chart labeled "How Well Do I Know These Words and Concepts?" from *Words, Words, Words* by Janet Allen
- Overhead transparency for three-column chart labeled "Asking Questions Before Reading, During the First Reading, and During the Second Reading"
- Strategy application notebooks

2: Asking Questions

Teaching Moves

Start-up/Connection

BUILDING BACKGROUND

- Ask a question to elicit students' prior knowledge about Columbus.
- Have students share their experiences with the topic.
- Brainstorm a variety of opinions about Christopher Columbus's influence in the New World. Include students' experiences and what they know through other means such as TV, movies, the Internet, and cultural connections.
- With students' input, draw a Venn diagram to categorize what they contribute about the Native Americans' perspective on Columbus's arrival in the New World and Columbus's perspective. Compare the similarities and differences in these two points of view.
- Provide comprehensible input about the topic: other books (such as *Encounter* by Jane Yolen), and television resources such as the Discovery Channel, the History Channel, and the National Geographic Channel.
- Relate the text directly to the topic by telling students, "There are a number of different opinions about the effect of Christopher Columbus's arrival on the Taino. As we read the history book, keep in mind that there is not just one point of view."
- As they read, compare what students learn about Christopher Columbus and the Taino with the Venn diagram they developed.

DEVELOPING VOCABULARY

Start by giving a textbook to each student in the small group. Before starting the lesson about Christopher Columbus, ask students to look through the lesson selection and identify words and concepts they need to have clarified. Chart their contributions on an overhead transparency using "How Well Do I Know These Words?" on page 127 of *Words, Words, Words* by Janet Allen as a guide. Write the word or concept as well as the sentence in which it is found.

Overhead Transparency

Vocabulary and Concepts to Clarify from "Columbus and the Taino"

Western Hemisphere: "On this fall morning, three ships landed near a small island in the Western Hemisphere."

Taino people: "The island was home to the Taino people."

Sailing under the flag of Spain: "A sea captain named Christopher Columbus, who was sailing under the flag of Spain, waded ashore.

How Well Do I Know These Words and Concepts?			
Don't know at all	**Have seen or heard—don't know meaning**	**I think I know the meaning**	**I know a meaning**
Taino people	Sailing under the flag of Spain	Western Hemisphere	Waded ashore

Discuss the words to be clarified, providing definitions as needed.

Give Information Explain to students that asking questions is important to developing an understanding of content-area and textbook reading. One way to do this is by asking questions before reading, during a first reading, and during a second reading (Harvey and Goudvis 2000, p. 270). Show students the three-column chart for asking questions that they will use when they read the textbook. Model your questions from before reading, during the first reading, and during the second reading. Write them on the overhead chart as you think aloud about your reading.

Overhead Transparency

Asking Questions About the History Textbook		
Questions Before Reading	**Questions During the First Reading**	**Questions During the Second Reading**
I understand that Christopher Columbus brought death and destruction to the Western Hemisphere. How did he do that?	Who are the Taino people?	Did the Taino people threaten Christopher Columbus and his ships? Was that why they took some as slaves?
Was Christopher Columbus a good or a bad influence?	Didn't Christopher Columbus land at Plymouth Rock? What was he doing landing near a small island?	What kind of disease was the worst for the Taino people?
Why do we celebrate Christopher Columbus Day?		How can a group of people like the Taino disappear?

Active Involvement "Working with a partner here at the table, you will read back through the section of the textbook that I just read. Talk about how I asked questions and wondered as I read and how that helped me understand what I was reading. Ask your own questions while you read. Share them with your partner and write them on the chart in your strategy application notebook. Remember to let your partner know how asking questions helped you understand the text."

Off You Go "Now you are ready to work on a new section of the textbook. Take a look at the next page. You'll work with your partner. First, write down the questions you have before you start reading. The first time you read through the section, write your questions in the column for the first reading. As you read through the text a second time, record your questions in the column for the second reading. When you have finished reading and recording, look back at your questions and see how they changed from column to column. Share what you have learned with your partner."

Instructional Materials

- *Tyrannosaurus Time* **(Just for a Day book) by Joanne Ryder**
- **Strategy application notebooks**

3: Visualizing—Creating Mental Images

Teaching Moves

Start-up/Connection

BUILDING BACKGROUND

- Ask a question to elicit students' prior knowledge about Tyrannosaurus rex.
- Have students share their experiences about the age of dinosaurs.
- Brainstorm characteristics for Tyrannosaurus rex such as habitat, food, and behavior. Include students' experiences and what they know through other means such as TV, movies, the Internet, and cultural connections.
- If necessary, provide comprehensible input about the topic, such as DVDs (*Walking with Dinosaurs* 2000 and *When Dinosaurs Roamed America* 2003 by the Discovery Channel), other books (*National Geographic Dinosaurs* by National Geographic), and television resources such as the Discovery Channel.
- Relate the text directly to the topic by telling students, "The book we will read takes us back to the age of dinosaurs."

DEVELOPING VOCABULARY

Start by taking a picture walk through the book *Tyrannosaurus Time* with a small group. As you move through the book, use vocabulary from the text to talk about the pictures. For example, on the second page of the story, it says, "You barely feel the sand rushing, brushing against your pebbly skin." Use the term *pebbly skin* as you talk about the pictures. Check with students to see if this is a concept they understand. Continue through the pictures, clarifying vocabulary from the book as needed.

Give Information Explain to students that visualizing and creating mental images as you read helps you understand the text. In this text students will visualize themselves as a Tyrannosuarus rex. Let students know that visualizing helps readers understand not only fiction but also informational text.

Active Involvement As you read aloud *Tyrannosaurus Time,* have students visualize themselves in the role of the girl or the boy at the beginning of the book. Have them share their mental images of what it was like during the time of Tyrannosaurus rex. Explain how readers use all their senses when they read. Encourage them to respond with, "I see...," "I hear...," "I can feel...," "I smell...," and "I can taste..." when they imagine themselves in the time of Tyrannosaurus rex. This allows them to interact with the text and show their understanding of it. Have students cite places in the text that helped them create their mental images. Talk about how the details and description in the writing help readers make mental images and see movies of the story in their minds. Student visualizations are shown in figures 6.6 and 6.7.

Off You Go After reading the story, provide opportunities for students to work with a partner to talk about and describe their visualizations of the book. Hand out the students' strategy application notebooks so they can draw their visualizations. Make available other titles from the Just for a Day series so students may continue to visualize. The series includes *Lizard in the Sun, Winter Whale, Shark in the Sea, White Bear, Ice Bear,* and *Jaguar in the Forest.*

figure 6.6 *David draws his mental image from the point of view of Tyrannosaurus rex.*

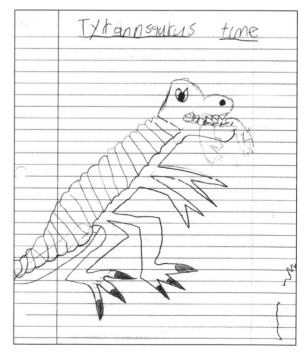

figure 6.7 *Bopa learns about the age of dinosaurs by visualizing.*

Instructional Materials

- *Grandma Fina and Her Wonderful Umbrellas* by Benjamin Alire Saenz
- Strategy application notebooks
- Overhead transparency for two-column chart labeled "Words in the Text/ Our Prediction of What Will Happen"

4: Inferring

Teaching Moves

Start-up/Connection Before reading aloud *Grandma Fina and Her Wonderful Umbrellas* with the students, take a look at the title, the cover, and the first few pages of the story. Have students predict what they think the story will be about. Encourage them to draw on their prior knowledge about grandmothers to predict.

Give Information Discuss with them how readers use words from the text to infer meaning and predict what will happen. As you read the selection aloud to students, model how you use words from the text to predict what will happen. Use the two-column chart to record your thinking. In the first column write the words from the text, and in the second column write your prediction.

Predicting (Inferring) About *Grandma Fina and Her Wonderful Umbrellas*	
Words in the Text	**Our Prediction of What Will Happen**
"She needs a new umbrella."	We predict that when Grandma Fina passes by Mrs. Byrd's house, Mrs. Byrd will ask what is wrong with her umbrella.
"And she kept walking down the street."	We predict Grandma Fina is going to keep walking by all her neighbors. She really likes to walk.
"'Nine umbrellas,' Gloria said. 'This is awful,' said Ruben."	We predict that because everyone gives Grandma Fina a new umbrella for her birthday, she will have a problem with too many umbrellas.
"Grandma Fina kept her favorite— her old yellow umbrella."	We predict she kept her old umbrella because she wants to save the new ones to use later.

Instructional Materials

- Comprehensible input about the rain forest
- *Kids Discover* magazine, *Rain Forests,* pages 6–7, "Plants of the Rain Forests"
- Overhead transparency for clarifying vocabulary and concepts
- Overhead transparency for FQR form
- Strategy application notebooks

Active Involvement As you read aloud from the text, encourage students to contribute their predictions along with the words in the text they used to make them. Students can also do their own two-column charts in their strategy application notebooks.

Off You Go As students read other selections, have them work with a partner to encourage conversations about predicting and to discuss how predicting helps them understand what they are reading. They can use the two-column chart as a model for predicting in their strategy application notebooks.

5: Determining Importance in Text

Teaching Moves

Start-up/Connection

BUILDING BACKGROUND

- Ask a question to elicit students' prior knowledge about the rain forest.

- Have students share their experiences with the rain forest.
- Brainstorm a variety of characteristics of rain forests, such as location, climate, animals, and plants. Include students' experiences and what they know through other means such as TV, movies, the Internet, and cultural connections.
- Provide comprehensible input about the topic, such as videos (*National Geographic: Really Wild Animals: Totally Tropical Rain Forest* 1994), other books (*The Great Kapok Tree: A Tale of the Amazon Rain Forest* by Lynne Cherry, and *One Day in the Tropical Rain Forest* by Jean Craighead George), and television resources such as the Discovery Channel, Animal Planet, and the National Geographic Channel.
- Relate the text, "Plants of the Rain Forests," directly to the topic by telling students, "There are many different aspects of the rain forest. The article we will be reading discusses plants of the rain forest."

DEVELOPING VOCABULARY

Before doing shared reading with the article, have students preview the two pages. Work together as a group to write words and concepts they need to have clarified on the overhead transparency. Have students use the context clues and their prior knowledge to predict what the words and concepts mean. Write their predictions on the transparency.

Overhead Transparency

Clarifying Vocabulary and Concepts About the Rain Forest		
Word or Concept	**Context for Word or Concept**	**Prediction for What It Means**
Despair	But don't despair.	Don't give up.
Intriguing	There are many intriguing and colorful plants and flowers that can be seen from the forest floor.	Strange and colorful plants and flowers.
Sky-high rain forest flowers	After you finish walking along the forest floor, you still may want to see and smell some of the sky-high rain forest flowers.	Really high up flowers in the rain forest.
Canopy	Once in the canopy, lianas may spread out intertwining among several trees.	The top?
Lianas	Once in the canopy, lianas may spread out intertwining among several trees.	Something like vines that wrap around?

Give Information Explain to students that you will read the text aloud as they follow along with their own copies (shared reading). Give each of them a copy of the article. As you read, think aloud as you identify facts about the rain forest. Make sure they understand that as they read, they should look for facts and then write down their questions and responses.

Overhead Transparency

FQR Chart for Determining Importance in Text		
Facts	**Questions**	**Responses**
"Most rain forest flowers are in the high tree branches."	Why do the flowers grow so high in the trees? Why don't they grow on the ground?	We think it is because they need the sunlight at the top because the rain forest has so many plants and the light can't come through.
"The ground in the rain forest is wet."	How much does it rain in the rain forest?	We imagine that it really rains a lot because the ground is wet and it is called the rain forest.
"Strangler figs grow high up in the canopy. When the fig reaches the ground, it sends roots into the soil. These roots eventually kill the host tree."	Why are they called strangler figs? How do they strangle the host tree with their roots?	We're thinking that these figs have very powerful roots and that they grab on to the host tree's roots and pull them out.
"The pitcher plant is a deadly trap! Its lovely fragrance attracts insects, which then fall into its container-shaped leaves and drown in digestive juices."	Why is a plant eating insects? How can it digest them? Does the plant get an upset stomach from the insects?	We think it is weird that the pitcher plant eats insects. It seems like this plant is a carnivore.

Active Involvement Encourage students to contribute facts from the article as you do the shared reading. Stop frequently and allow students to talk to a partner about the facts they are finding, their questions, and their responses.

Off You Go Have students read through another article in the magazine *Rain Forests* and work with a partner to record their facts, questions, and responses. Encourage them to use their strategy application notebooks for the FQR chart.

6: Synthesizing

Teaching Moves

Start-up/Connection This lesson will take several weeks. The idea with small-group inquiry projects is that working in a group acts as a scaffold as you gradually release responsibility to students. To provide background knowledge about inquiry projects in science, give students an overview of what they will be expected to do during the project. They will work with a group to select a topic, choose a question, do research, and make a final presentation. After the explanation, have students talk with a partner to demonstrate an understanding of what they will be doing. Work together to answer students' questions about the project.

To give students a little more information that might help them make wise topic choices and prime the pump for their own questions, we provide both a little bit of information on what the topic is about, and a hook that would draw students in to the topic. For example, for Systems in Living Things, we have our students brainstorm about systems that they already know, such as the bus system, the water system, and the air-conditioning system. Then we draw them in to a discussion about living things and systems. This leads us to a series of questions: What is the digestive system? What is the respiratory system? What is the circulatory system? To draw them in further and get them interested, we ask questions such as: "What happens to your food after you eat it? How does air move in and out of your body as you breathe? Ever wondered where your blood goes after it leaves your heart?"

Give Information Give students topics to choose from that match the science standards. Have the small group work together to choose one topic for their project. (Juli's group was studying Systems in Living Things, and they chose the circulatory system for their small-group inquiry project.) Encourage students to use sticky notes to record their questions about their topics. In addition, they can use the "I wonder. . ." pages in their strategy application notebooks to record their wonderings about the topic they have chosen.

Student Questions About the Circulatory System

Why do we have veins?
Why do the veins change colors?
Why do people have different blood types?
Do animals have the same blood as people and if so, why?
How does blood keep us alive?
Why are horses hot blooded?
Why do people's noses bleed?
How do you make blood inside your body?
Why is blood red?
Why do we have a system inside of us?

Once every group chooses a question and does some wondering about its topic, the research part of the inquiry begins. Limit the number of resources for this group project to help students focus on the information they can learn about their topic. Explain that students will use three of the same resources. They will use the online student magazines such as *Kids Discover* magazine, *Blood,* to gather some basic facts. Then they will use the science textbook to find out what connections their topic and their questions have to their textbook. Finally, they will use the CD-ROM of the *World Book Encyclopedia* to

Instructional Materials

- Science textbooks
- Online magazines for students
  - *Kids Discover* magazine http://www.kidsdiscover.com
  - *Time for Kids* magazine http://www.timeforkids.com
  - *National Geographic Kids* magazine http://www.nationalgeographic.com/ngkids/
  - *National Geographic Explorer* magazine http://magma.nationalgeographic.com/ngexplorer/
- Science standards
- Strategy application notebooks
- Chart paper for final presentations
- Synthesizing pyramid project sheet
- *Nonfiction Matters* by Stephanie Harvey

gather even more information and gain experience using a reference. After that, if they have more time, they can search for their topic on the Internet or look for information in other places such as the school library. At each point in the inquiry project, students will need teacher modeling to understand what they are to do. The teacher may do her own project for the purposes of modeling for the students.

Additional tools to aid students' research include the following:

- Computers
- The Internet
- Word processing software
- Highlighters and sticky notes
- Clipboards
- A variety of paper, including graph paper
- Chart paper, transparencies, and markers

Active Involvement To help students understand and make sense of the information they gather, break the topic down into smaller pieces based on their questions. Have each student pick one question to investigate.

Questions Students Chose to Investigate About the Circulatory System

Why do the veins change colors?
Why do people have different blood types?
How does blood keep us alive?
How do you make blood inside your body?
Why do people's noses bleed?

Then help the students organize their questions into sections. Since they are working on this project as a group, each member is responsible for one section of the project based on their question about the topic. See figures 6.8 and 6.9.

To give students a more authentic experience as investigators, include a choice of ways for them to obtain information from both primary and secondary sources. They might try the following:

- Interviewing
- Creating and administering questionnaires and surveys
- Note taking
- Viewing or listening to CD-ROMs, videotapes, and audiotapes

As the last part of the project, each group prepares a presentation. They can do their presentation for another small group to provide a low-anxiety, risk-free environment for using oral language. Each member of the group is responsible for a different section, based on their individual questions, and then the group as a whole decides on the sequence in which the sections will be presented. Provide each group with a large piece of chart paper so they can prepare a chart for their presentation. The purpose of the presentation is to give students a chance to teach others what they have learned from investigating their questions.

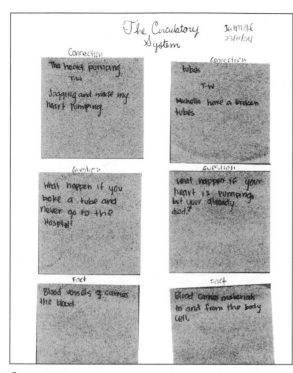

figure 6.8 *Jeannie uses strategies as she thinks about the circulatory system.*

figure 6.9 *Jonathan organizes sticky notes with his connections, questions, and facts.*

Synthesizing Frame for Inquiry Questions

I first thought this...
But then I learned...
Next I learned...
But this changed everything because...
This is way different from what I thought at the beginning. My thinking changed because...

Off You Go During the project, have students keep track of where their thinking about how their question changes. Have students use the synthesizing frame to scaffold their synthesizing. Confer with students as the project ends to have them explain how their thinking changed. Use the frame as a guide for the individual conferences about synthesizing.

Jose's synthesizing frame for "Why do people's noses bleed?"

I first thought this: that people's noses bleed because they get hit with a ball in the face or someone punches them in the nose.

But then I learned that in your nose there are little capillaries filled with blood that are very close to the surface.

Next I learned that sometimes people get nosebleeds in really dry or hot weather.

But this changed everything because when I interviewed the nurse about my question, she gave me information about why your nose bleeds and a paper that tells you what to do if your nose is bleeding. You shouldn't lie down. Just put your head back and pinch your nose to stop the blood.

This is way different from what I thought at the beginning. My thinking changed because I learned that sometimes the inside of your nose gets dry and the skin cracks and the capillaries are close to the surface and so they bleed.

Books for Teaching Strategies to Younger English Language Learners

Advanced Stage

Making Connections

Dia's Story Cloth: The Hmong People's Journey of Freedom by Dia Cha
Every Living Thing by Cynthia Rylant
Jingle Dancer by Cynthia Leitich Smith
Silent Lotus by Jeanne E. Lee
Snapshots from the Wedding by Gary Soto

Asking Questions

. . . If You Grew Up With George Washington by Ruth Belov Gross
Something Permanent by Cynthia Rylant and Walker Evans
The New Way Things Work by David McCauley
What Makes an Ocean Wave? Questions and Answers About Oceans and Ocean Life by Melvin and Gilda Berger

Visualizing

Joyful Noise: Poems for Two Voices by Paul Fleischmann
Panther, Shadow of the Swamp by Jonathon London
Come With Me: Poems for a Journey by Naomi Shihab Nye
Tyrannosaurus Time (Just for a Day book) by Joanne Ryder
Wings by Christopher Myers
My Name is Jorge: On Both Sides of the River, Poems in English and Spanish by Jane Medina

Inferring

Annie and the Old One by Miska Miles
Grandma Fina and Her Wonderful Umbrellas by Benjamin Alire Saenz
My Freedom Trip: A Child's Escape from North Korea by Frances and Ginger Park

The Frog Prince Continued by John Scieszka
The Stinky Cheese Man and Other Fairly Stupid Tales by John Scieszka
The True Story of the Three Little Pigs! by John Scieszka
The Three Little Javelinas by Susan Lowell

Determining Importance in Text

Kids Discover magazine
  http://www.kidsdiscover.com
Time for Kids magazine
  http://www.timeforkids.com
National Geographic Kids magazine
  http://www.nationalgeographic.com/ngkids/
National Geographic Explorer magazine
  http://magma.nationalgeographic.com/ngexplorer/
Sports Illustrated for Kids magazine
  http://www.sikids.com/

Synthesizing

My Diary From Here to There by Amanda Irma Perez
Ruby Lu, Brave and True by Lenore Look
Hiroshima by Lawrence Yep
The Circuit: Stories from the Life of a Migrant Child by
  Francisco Jimenez
The Pot That Juan Built by Nancy Andrews Goebel

Older English Language Learners in Real Time

Viviana is engrossed in research for her inquiry project. To get started, she chooses a question to investigate. But, as time goes on, she's finding she has other questions. She's part of a small group of English Language Learners who are working with Juli to plan and organize their projects.

"My first question was, How do you stay safe during dangerous weather?" Viviana says. "But now I have lots more questions like, Why does there have to be a tornado? and Why are tornadoes so scary?"

Others in Viviana's small group are also investigating and researching questions. They've chosen How do astronomers learn about space? What is a living thing? and Why does air move?

As one question leads to another, kids begin to realize how important it is to ask questions and wonder about what you are reading if you want to understand and learn new information. One brave soul explains it this way: "At first, I was reading a book about space and I had a question: How many planets are there in the solar system? But then I started wondering about the

Internet. They said there might be ten planets, not nine. So I did more research, and I learned that Pluto has a moon called Charon and that some people think it may really be another planet."

Juli watches with interest as this student negotiates his way by asking more questions. He's developing a deeper understanding and learning that not all questions have answers. "I don't think they really know how many planets are in our solar system," he comments, referring to the differing opinions of astronomers. "Some of them think that Pluto is a bipolar planet. What's a bipolar planet? And some of them think that Charon is the tenth planet. They need to do more research."

It's easy to see how these students can ask questions that encourage more research and deepen their understandings. Asking questions leads them to learn more about English as well as to a deeper understanding about what they are reading.

Lesson Plans for Older English Language Learners

1: Making Connections

Teaching Moves

Instructional Materials

▪ *The Caged Birds of Phnom Penh* by Frederick Lipp
▪ Sticky notes
▪ Overhead transparency for two-column making-connections chart

Start-up/Connection Before reading, discuss with the students what they know about making wishes. Have students share their background knowledge. Draw on traditions for making wishes such as wishing wells, blowing out candles on a birthday cake, throwing coins in a fountain, and wishing upon a star.

Give Information As you read aloud *The Caged Birds of Phnom Penh,* think aloud about your own connections. "This reminds me of . . . and that helps me understand this selection better because. . . ." As you read the first half of the book with the students, write your own connections on the overhead transparency for the two-column chart as a model.

Active Involvement Provide copies of the story for each student. Tell students, "Working with a partner, you will read through the rest of the story. As you read, stop and talk about the connections you are making and why they help you understand what you are reading. Be sure to share your connections with your partner. Remember to let your partner know what kind of a connection it is—text-to-self, text-to-text, or text-to-world—where you make the connection in the text, and how making the connection helps you understand the text. Record your connections on the two-column chart in your strategy application notebook."

Overhead Transparency

Making Connections for *The Caged Birds of Phnom Penh*	
Connection	**Evidence/Words from the Text**
This reminds me of when we have smog in the air, and it's hard to breathe.	"The yellow winds grew gray. Gray winds were difficult to breathe."
This reminds me of the Buddhist temple near our school where the monks live. But they don't have a market there where they sell things.	"Here by the Buddhist temple, merchants were setting up shop."
This reminds me of when I made a wish and blew out the candles on my birthday cake. I thought that I would get my wish if I blew out all the candles.	"I want to set a little bird free so my wishes for my family will come true."
Last Christmas I wished for skates and instead I got a scooter, but that was OK.	"Answers to wishes rarely come in the manner we expect."
This reminds me of how you never know what a new day will bring.	"The form they would take was as uncertain as the new day."

Off You Go When students are reading other texts, encourage them to use the two-column chart for making connections to record their thinking in their strategy application notebooks. Talking with a partner about the connections helps them develop oral language and deepen their understanding of what they are reading.

2: Asking Questions

Teaching Moves

Start-up/Connection

BUILDING BACKGROUND

- Ask a question to elicit students' prior knowledge about the ancient Romans.
- Have students share their experiences with the topic.
- Brainstorm a variety of aspects of the ancient Romans, such as how they lived, family life, education, and entertainment. Include students' experiences and what they know through other means such as TV, movies, the Internet, and cultural connections.
- With student input, draw a graphic organizer to categorize what students contribute. We suggest using the B-K-W-L-Q chart from Janet Allen's *Tools for Teaching Content Literacy.*

Instructional Materials

- B-K-W-L-Q chart from Janet Allen's *Tools for Teaching Content Literacy*
- Comprehensible input about the ancient Romans
- Copies of *How Would You Survive as an Ancient Roman?* by Anita Ganeri
- Sticky notes (thick questions) and sticky flags (thin questions)
- Overhead transparency for "How Well Do I Know These Words?" from *Words, Words, Words* by Janet Allen, page 128
- Overhead transparency for "Thick and Thin Questions" chart
- Strategy application notebooks

- Provide comprehensible input about the topic such as videos (*History Channel Presents: Ancient Rome* 2005 and *National Geographic's In the Shadow of Vesuvius* 1983), other books (*Ancient Rome: Eyewitness Books* by Simon James), and television resources such as the Discovery Channel, the History Channel, and the National Geographic Channel.
- Relate the text directly to the topic by telling students, "The ancient Romans did many of the same things we do, but in very different ways. The section of the book we will be reading gives information about education in ancient Rome."
- Compare what they learn about ancient Rome as they read to the graphic organizer they developed.

DEVELOPING VOCABULARY

Begin by giving a copy of the book *How Would You Survive as an Ancient Roman?* to each student. Before starting the lesson, ask students to look through the selection about education, "What Would You Learn?" on pages 26 and 27, and identify words and concepts they need to have clarified. After you discuss the words and concepts, have students sort their contributions on an overhead transparency using "How Well Do I Know These Words?" on page 128 of *Words, Words, Words* by Janet Allen. Write the word or concept as well as the sentence in which it is found.

How Well Do I Know These Words?		
I still need help finding a meaning for this word	**I think I know the meaning**	**I know a meaning**
Philosophers—"Later, you will study the works of Greek and Roman playwrights, poets, and philosophers."	*Midday*—"If you go to school, lessons last from dawn to midday."	*Preparation*—"If you have sisters their lessons will soon stop so your mother can teach them household duties in preparation for marriage."
	Rhetoric—"If you intend following a career in politics or the law, it is essential to learn rhetoric, the art of public speaking."	*Presenting*—"He will teach you how to write speeches and the most persuasive ways of presenting them."
		Papyrus—"authors write on long scrolls made from papyrus (an Egyptian reed) or parchment made from kidskin."

Give Information Explain to students that understanding how to ask different kinds of questions is important to developing an understanding of content-area reading. One way to talk about this is to refer to thick versus thin questions (Harvey and Goudvis 2000, p. 89). Thick questions often begin with *Why, How,* or *I wonder.* Thin questions often have yes/no answers or short answers.

As you read aloud the selection from the textbook, think aloud about your questions and wonderings. "As I was reading, I was asking questions and wondering about…and that helps me understand this selection because…." Record your questions and wonderings. Write thick questions on sticky notes labeled "Thick" and thin questions on sticky flags labeled "Thin." Use the stickies to mark the book. Use the Thick and Thin Questions chart to organize your questions according to "thick" or "thin."

Thick and Thin Questions for *How Would You Survive as an Ancient Roman?*	
Thick Questions	**Thin Questions**
Why?	*Yes/no answers*
Why didn't the ancient Romans have pencils like us?	Did they have books?
	Did they have school like us?
Why did they use the scrolls?	Did they have tables and desks?
How?	Did they wear uniforms to school?
How do they use an abacus for math?	If they wore uniforms, did they buy their uniforms at school?
How can you count on an abacus?	
I wonder	*Short answers*
I wonder what they did at school for history.	Who was the principal?
I wonder what history they studied.	

Active Involvement "Working with a partner, you will read through the next section of the book. Talk about your questions and organize them on a Thick and Thin Questions chart in your strategy application notebook. Use sticky notes and sticky flags to tab your questions if it helps you understand which are thick questions and which are thin questions. We're doing this so we can learn how to ask high-level questions (thick questions)."

Off You Go Provide more opportunities for students to use sticky notes and sticky flags to mark their thick and thin questions as they read. Encourage them to organize their questions on a Thick and Thin Questions chart in their strategy application notebooks. Talk with students about the importance of asking high-level questions.

Instructional Materials

- Cool Salsa, Poems on Growing Up Latino in the United States ed. by Lori M. Carlson
- Copies of two poems from the Carlson book: "Good Hot Dog" by Sandra Cisneros and "Mango Juice" by Pat Mora
- Strategy application notebooks

3: Visualizing—Creating Mental Images

Teaching Moves

Start-up/Connection

- Ask a question to elicit students' prior knowledge about growing up in the United States.
- Have students share their experiences about growing up in the United States.
- Ask questions to prompt them to think about where they grew up. "Where were you born? Did you grow up there? How long have you lived in the United States? How long have you lived in this city?" Students will probably have a wide variety of answers. Although they are older and at the advanced stage, some of them may be new arrivals, some might have lived in another part of the United States, and some may have lived where they are so long that they won't have much memory of growing up elsewhere.
- Directly relate the poems the students will be reading to the topic of growing up in the United States by telling students, "We are going to read poems about what it is like to grow up Latino in the United States."

DETERMINING IMPORTANCE IN TEXT

Talk with students about what it is like for them growing up. Discuss the similarities and differences between growing up in the United States and growing up in other countries.

Give Information Explain to students that visualizing and creating mental images while reading helps readers understand the text. Let students know that visualizing helps you understand not only fiction but also poetry. As you do shared reading with the two poems, have students visualize what the poems are saying. As a model, stop reading from time to time and think aloud about what you are visualizing about the poems.

Active Involvement After you model by thinking aloud as you read, have students share their mental images of what they visualized. Explain how readers use all of their senses when they read. Encourage them to respond with, I see..., I hear..., I can feel..., I smell..., and/or I can taste.... This allows them to interact with the poems and show their understanding. Have students cite places in the poems that helped them create mental images. Talk about how the details and description in the writing help readers see mental images of the poems in their mind. See figures 6.10, 6.11, and 6.12.

Off You Go After reading the poems, provide opportunities for students to work with a partner to talk about and describe their visualizations of the poems. Have students draw their visualizations of the poems in their strategy application notebooks.

figure 6.10 *Veronica keeps track of her mental images in her notebook.*

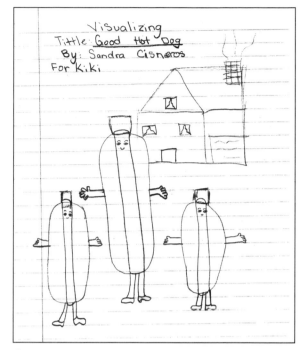

figure 6.11 *Mary's visualization of "Good Hot Dog" by Sandra Cisneros.*

figure 6.12 *Oscar makes a movie in his mind of "Mango Juice" using his strategy application notebook.*

Instructional Materials

- *A Gift from Papá Diego* by Benjamin Alire Saenz
- Strategy application notebooks
- Overhead transparency for three-column chart labeled "Words in the Text/Prediction/Confirmed or Contradicted" (Harvey and Goudvis 2000, p. 277)

4: Inferring

Teaching Moves

Start-up/Connection Talk with students about what they know about grandfathers. Have them draw on their background knowledge to predict what this book, *A Gift from Papá Diego,* will be about. Let them know that Papá Diego is a grandfather.

Give Information It's important for students to know that readers use words in the text to predict what will happen. They also need to know that after readers make predictions, they should read farther to see if their predictions are confirmed or contradicted by the text.

Active Involvement As you read the text aloud, think aloud to model how to use the words in the text to make predictions. Use the three-column chart to record your thinking. In the first column write the words from the text, in the second column write your prediction, and in the third column, as you continue to read, add whether it is confirmed or contradicted. Encourage students to add their own predictions to the overhead transparency.

Overhead Transparency

Predicting (Inferring) About *A Gift from Papá Diego*		
Words in the Text	**Prediction**	**Confirmed or Contradicted**
"But they lived in different countries, and Little Diego did not see his grandfather very often."	We predict that he is in the United States and his grandpa is in Mexico.	*Confirmed* He lives in Chihuahua, Mexico.
"Mijo, Papá Diego likes living in Mexico — it's his home. He wouldn't like living here."	We predict that he doesn't want to live in the United States because he doesn't know where the streets are and everything is different.	We can't confirm or contradict this prediction.
"He even practiced his Spanish every day just in case his Papá Diego . . ."	We predict that his grandfather speaks only Spanish.	*Confirmed* He speaks only Spanish.

Off You Go As students read other stories, have them work with a partner to encourage conversation about predicting and inferring. Have them record their predictions in their strategy application notebooks. They can use the three-column chart as a model for their notebooks.

5: Determining Importance in Text

Teaching Moves

Start-up/Connection

BUILDING BACKGROUND

- Ask a question to elicit students' prior knowledge about the Civil War.
- Have students share their experiences with the topic.
- Brainstorm about the Civil War (who fought, how they fought, why they were fighting, and so on). Include students' experiences and what they know through other means such as TV, movies, the Internet, and cultural connections.
- Provide comprehensible input about the Civil War, such as videos/DVDs (*The Civil War*—A Film by Ken Burns), Web sites, other books (such as *Civil War: Eyewitness Books* by John Stanchak and *The Boys' War: Confederate and Union Soldiers Talk About the Civil War* by Jim Murphy), and television resources such as the Discovery Channel, the History Channel, and the National Geographic Channel.
- Relate the text directly to the Civil War by telling students, "The article we will be reading discusses the start of the Civil War."

DEVELOPING VOCABULARY

Begin by giving a copy of *War, Terrible War, A History of Us* to each student. Ask students to look through the selection "The War Begins" and identify words and concepts that they need to have clarified. Chart their contributions on an overhead transparency using "How Well Do I Know These Words?" on page 128 of *Words, Words, Words* by Janet Allen. Write the word or concept as well as the sentence in which it is found.

How Well Do I Know These Words?		
I still need help finding a meaning for this word	**I think I know the meaning**	**I know a meaning**
Confederate —"General P. T. Beauregard led the Confederate attack on Fort Sumter."	*Volley* —"We…fired a volley, and saw the Rebels running"	*Seige guns* —"Seige guns, like this 15-inch cannon…"
Northern soldiers —"The Northern soldiers, who had planned to fight on to Richmond…"	*Waterfront*— "the Charleston waterfront"	*Railroad junction* —"the place where two railroad lines met"

Instructional Materials

- ☐ "The War Begins," in *War, Terrible War* from the series *A History of Us* by Joy Hakim
- ☐ Overhead transparency for "How Well Do I Know These Words?" from *Words, Words, Words* by Janet Allen, page 128
- ☐ Overhead transparency for two-column chart labeled "Important Event/ Evidence from the Text"
- ☐ Strategy application notebooks

Give Information Explain to students that you will read the text aloud as they follow along with their own copies (shared reading). As you read, think aloud about the important events in the book. Make sure students understand that as they read they should look for important events and evidence in the text. Show them the two-column chart on the overhead transparency that you will use to record the events and the evidence from the text (Harvey and Goudvis 2000, p. 282).

Determining Importance in Text	
Important Event	**Evidence from the Text**
Start of the Civil War	Southern guns fired on U.S. troops stationed at Fort Sumter, Charleston, South Carolina.
First big battle of the Civil War	It was fought at Manassas, near a muddy stream known as Bull Run, and won by the South.
People came to watch the battle at Manassas.	People from Washington thought war was entertaining, like a TV show. They brought picnic baskets and came to sit and eat and watch the battle.
It was a messy, hard-fought battle.	The soldiers on both sides were untrained and didn't know what they were doing.

Active Involvement When you find an important event as you read aloud, point out the evidence from the text and write it on the two-column chart. Encourage students to contribute their own events and evidence from the text. Stop frequently and allow students to talk to a partner about what they find.

Off You Go Have students read through the next article and work with a partner to record the important events and the evidence from the text in their strategy application notebooks. They can use the two-column chart. Also, have them use a dictionary and/or thesaurus to look up definitions for any vocabulary and/or concepts they still need to clarify.

6: Synthesizing

Teaching Moves

Start-up/Connection

BUILDING BACKGROUND

- Ask a question to elicit students' prior knowledge about the topic of children and war. For example, "What do you think a child's life would be like in a country during a war?"

Instructional Materials

- Comprehensible input about Sarajevo and war
- *Zlata's Diary: A Child's Life in Sarajevo* by Zlata Filipovic
- Sticky notes
- Strategy application notebooks
- Overhead transparency for synthesizing frame

- Have students share their experiences with the topic.
- Brainstorm about the effects of war on children, families, education, transportation, food, and so on. Include students' experiences and what they know through other means such as TV, movies, the Internet, and cultural connections.
- Provide comprehensible input about the topic, such as other books (for example, *Anne Frank: The Diary of a Young Girl* by Anne Frank and *Family from Bosnia* by Julia Waterlow), and television resources such as the Discovery Channel, the History Channel, and the National Geographic Channel.
- Directly relate the text, *Zlata's Diary: A Child's Life in Sarajevo,* to the topic of children and war by telling students, "The selections we will read are from a diary by Zlata, a young girl who lived in Sarajevo. The diary tells what it was like for her and her family as their city became involved in war."

Give Information Explain to students that they will be reading selections that Zlata wrote in her diary when she lived in Sarajevo. They will use the synthesizing frame to help them understand how their thinking changes as they read.

Synthesizing Frame

Before I started reading, I thought *Zlata's Diary* was about...
Then after we read a little, I thought it was going to be about...because I read....
But then I read something different about...so now I'm changing my thinking.
My synthesis has changed because....

Active Involvement To model synthesizing, read aloud several selections from the diary and think aloud about how your thinking is changing as you read. Have students use sticky notes to mark the text. As a reminder, have them write, "I'm thinking that..." on the sticky note. Stop frequently to ask students where their thinking is changing. Have them read aloud the place in the text where they placed the sticky notes and explain how their thinking changed. To model synthesizing, use the synthesizing frame and work with the students to write the frame on the overhead transparency. When finished, students can place their sticky notes in their strategy application notebooks and use the synthesizing frame to record their thinking.

Small-Group Synthesizing Frame for Zlata's Diary

Before we started reading, we thought *Zlata's Diary* was about a little girl who wrote a diary about her boyfriends and all the dates she had and the fun things that she did in her life.

Then after we read a little, we thought she was going to write about living in Sarajevo because we read that Zlata lived there with her family.

But then we read something different about Sarajevo. Zlata said that a medical student had been killed marching peacefully across the Vrbanja bridge and that nothing there was normal. So now we're changing our thinking.

Our synthesis has changed because we used to think that she had a happy life, but now we know that there was a war in Sarajevo. It was very frightening for Zlata's family and the other people who lived there.

Off You Go Allow students to read additional selections from *Zlata's Diary*. Have them read along with a partner to talk about their synthesizing and indicate the places in the diary where their thinking changes. Students can also add their synthesizing to their strategy application notebooks.

Books for Teaching Strategies to Older English Language Learners

Advanced Stage

Making Connections

The Caged Birds of Phnom Penh by Frederick Lipp
Ruby's Wish by Shirin Yim Bridges
Kite Fighters by Linda Sue Park
Woman Hollering Creek and Other Stories by Sandra Cisneros
A Summer Life by Gary Soto

Asking Questions

How Would You Survive as an Ancient Roman? by Anita Ganeri
New York Times articles at http://www.nytimes.com/
So You Want to Be President? by Judith George
"How Stuff Works," Web site for asking questions at http://www
   .howstuffworks.com/
*Ben Franklin's Almanac, Being a True Account of the True Gentleman's
   Life* by Candace Fleming

Visualizing

A Suitcase of Seaweed and Other Poems by Janet Wong
Cool Salsa: Poems on Growing Up Latino in the United States edited by
   Lori M. Carlson
Wáchale: Poetry and Prose About Growing Up Latino in America ed. by
   Ilan Stavans
Laughing Out Loud, I Fly (poems) by Juan Felipe Herrera
Salting the Ocean: 100 Poems by Young Poets ed. by Naomi Shihab Nye

Inferring

A Gift From Papá Diego by Benjamin Alire Saenz
*Between Earth and Sky: Legends of Native American Sacred Place*s by
  Joseph Bruchac
The Man Who Walked Between the Towers by Mordecai Gerstein
The Moon Lady by Amy Tan

Determining Importance in Text

Kids Discover magazine
  http://www.kidsdiscover.com
Time for Kids magazine
  http://www.timeforkids.com
National Geographic Kids magazine
  http://www.nationalgeographic.com/ngkids/
National Geographic Explorer magazine
  http://magma.nationalgeographic.com/ngexplorer/
Sports Illustrated for Kids magazine
  http://www.sikids.com/
A History of Us (ten-book set) by Joy Hakim

Synthesizing

Anne Frank: The Diary of a Young Girl by Anne Frank
Coolies by Yin
Family from Bosnia by Julia Waterlow
Harvesting Hope: The Story of Cesar Chavez by Kathleen Krull
Salsa Stories by Lulu Delacre
Zlata's Diary by Zlata Filipovic

RESOURCES AND REFERENCES

Web Sites

"Growing Up Asian in America" (annual award-winning art, poetry, and essays by Asian American students grades K–12).
http://www.asianpacificfund.org/awards/guaa/program.php

"How Stuff Works," Web site for asking questions.
http://www.howstuffworks.com/

Collection of predictable texts.
http://www.monroe.lib.in.us/childrens/predict.html
Monroe County Public Library, Monroe County, Indiana

International Children's Digital Library, A project of the University of Maryland and the Internet Archive.
http://www.icdlbooks.org/

Student Magazines

Kids Discover magazine
http://www.kidsdiscover.com

National Geographic Kids
http://www.nationalgeographic.com/ngkids/

National Geographic Explorer
http://magma.nationalgeographic.com/ngexplorer/

Sports Illustrated for Kids
http://www.sikids.com/

Time for Kids
http://www.timeforkids.com

Videos and DVDs

Crazy Horse and the Lakota Sioux Indians. VHS. 2004. New Dimension Media. Chicago: Questar Inc.

History Channel Presents: Ancient Rome. DVD. 2005. A&E Home Video: The History Channel.

National Geographic: Really Wild Animals: Totally Tropical Rain Forest. VHS. 1994. Sony Pictures. Washington, DC: National Geographic.

National Geographic's In the Shadow of Vesuvius. DVD. 1997. Washington, DC: National Geographic.

The Civil War—A Film by Ken Burns. DVD. 2004. Hollywood, CA: Paramount Home Video.

Walking with Dinosaurs. DVD. 2000. BBC Video.

When Dinosaurs Roamed America. DVD. 2003. Artisan Entertainment. The Discovery Channel.

Wolves: A Legend Returns to Yellowstone. VHS. 1999. Washington, DC: National Geographic.

Professional Literature

Allen, Janet. 1999. *Words, Words, Words: Teaching Vocabulary in Grades 4–12.* Portland, ME: Stenhouse.

——. 2002. *On the Same Page: Shared Reading Beyond the Primary Grades.* Portland, ME: Stenhouse.

——. 2004. *Tools for Teaching Content Literacy.* Portland, ME: Stenhouse.

Calkins, Lucy. 2001. *The Art of Teaching Reading.* New York: Longman.

Clay, Marie. 1998. *By Different Paths to Common Outcomes.* York, ME: Stenhouse.

Cummins, James. 2000. *Language, Power, and Pedagogy: Bilingual Children in the Crossfire.* Clevedon, UK: Multilingual Matters.

Diller, Debbie. 2003. *Literacy Work Stations.* Portland, ME: Stenhouse.

——. 2005. *Practice with Purpose: Literacy Work Stations for Grades 3–6.* Portland, ME: Stenhouse.

Echevarria, Jana, MaryEllen Vogt, and Deborah J. Short. 2003. *Making Content Comprehensible for English Language Learners: The SIOP Model, Second Edition.* Needham Heights, MA: Allyn and Bacon.

Einhorn, Carole. 2002. "The Architecture of Teaching" http://www.dist428.dekalb.k12.il.us/admin/personl/mentor/architec.pdf.

Fay, Kathleen, Suzanne Whaley, and Joann Portalupi. 2004. *Becoming One Community: Reading and Writing with English Language Learners.* Portland, ME: Stenhouse.

Freeman, Yvonne and David Freeman. 2004. "Connecting Students to Culturally Relevant Texts." April/May 2004. *Talking Points,* Volume 15, Number 2. NCTE.

Hakuta, Kenji and Diane August, editors. 1998. *Educating Language-Minority Children*. Washington, DC: National Academy Press. http://www.nap.edu/books/0309064147/html/.

Harvey, Stephanie. 1998. *Nonfiction Matters: Reading, Writing, and Research in Grades 3–8*. Portland, ME: Stenhouse.

Harvey, Stephanie and Anne Goudvis. 2000. *Strategies That Work: Teaching Comprehension to Enhance Understanding*. Portland, ME: Stenhouse.

Keene, Ellin and Susan Zimmermann. 1997. *Mosaic of Thought: Teaching Comprehension in a Reader's Workshop*. Portsmouth, NH: Heinemann.

Kendall, Juli. 2001–2005. "Juli Kendall's Reading/Writing Workshop Journals." Little Switzerland, NC: MiddleWeb. http://www.middleweb.com/mw/workshop/R_W_Project.html.

Krashen, Stephen D. 1996. *The Natural Approach: Language Acquisition in the Classroom*. Tarset, Northumberland, UK: Bloodaxe Books, Ltd.

———. 2003. *Explorations in Language Acquisition and Use*. Portsmouth, NH: Heinemann.

———. 2004. *The Power of Reading (2nd Edition): Insights from the Research*. Portsmouth, NH: Heinemann.

Mendoza, Jeanne and Debbie Reese. 2001. "Examining Multicultural Picture Books for the Early Childhood Classroom: Possibilities and Pitfalls." University of Illinois at Urbana–Champaign. http://ceep.crc.uiuc.edu/pubs/katzsym/mendoza-reese.html.

Miller, Debbie. 2002. *Reading with Meaning: Teaching Comprehension in the Primary Grades*. Portland, ME: Stenhouse.

NWREL. 2003. "By Request . . . Strategies and Resources for Mainstream Teachers of English Language Learners." Northwest Regional Educational Laboratory. http://www.nwrel.org/request/2003may/.

Pearson, P. David and M.C. Gallagher. 1983. "The Instruction of Reading Comprehension." *Contemporary Educational Psychology* 8: 317–344.

Taberski, Sharon. 2000. *On Solid Ground: Strategies for Teaching Reading K–3*. Portsmouth, NH: Heinemann.

Tovani, Cris. 2000. *I Read It But I Don't Get It: Comprehension Strategies for Adolescent Readers*. Portland, ME: Stenhouse.

———. 2004. *Do I Really Have to Teach Reading? Content Comprehension, Grades 6–12*. Portland, ME: Stenhouse.

Valdés, Guadalupe. 2001. *Learning and Not Learning English: Latino Students in American Schools*. New York: Teachers College Press.

Children's Literature

2003. *Farm Animals* (DK Lift-the-Flap). New York: DK Publishing.

Ada, Alma Flor. 1997. *Gathering the Sun: An Alphabet in English and Spanish*. New York: Rayo.

——. 2002. *I Love Saturdays y domingos*. New York: Atheneum.

Alarcon, Francisco X. 1997. *Laughing Tomatoes and Other Spring Poems*. San Francisco: Children's Book Press.

——. 1998. *From the Belly Button of the Moon and Other Summer Poems*. San Francisco: Children's Book Press.

——. 1999. *Angels Ride Bikes and Other Fall Poems*. San Francisco: Children's Book Press.

——. 2001. *Iguanas in the Snow and Other Winter Poems*. San Francisco: Children's Book Press.

Altman, Linda. 1995. *Amelia's Road*. New York: Lee & Low Books.

Anaya, Rudolfo. 2000. *Roadrunner's Dance*. New York: Hyperion.

Anno, Mitsumasa. 1986. *Anno's Counting Book*. New York: HarperTrophy.

Anzaldua, Gloria. 2001. *Prietita and the Ghost Woman*. San Francisco: Children's Book Press.

Argueta, Jorge. 2001. *A Movie in My Pillow*. San Francisco: Children's Book Press.

——. 2003. *Xochiti and the Flowers*. San Francisco: Children's Book Press.

Arnosky, Jim. 2002. *All About Rattlesnakes*. New York: Scholastic.

——. 2003. *All About Sharks*. New York: Scholastic.

Baker, Jeannie. 2004. *Home*. New York: Greenwillow Books.

Ballard, Robert D. 1993. *Finding the Titanic*. Hello Reader series. New York: Scholastic.

Bang, Molly. 1996. *The Grey Lady and the Strawberry Snatcher*. New York: Aladdin.

Banyai, Istvan. 1998. *Zoom*. New York: Puffin Books.

——. 1998. *Re-Zoom*. New York: Puffin Books.

Barrett, Judi. 2001. *Which Witch Is Which?* New York: Atheneum Books for Young Readers.

Barrett, Paul. 2001. *National Geographic Dinosaurs*. Washington, DC: National Geographic.

Baylor, Byrd. 1998. *I'm in Charge of Celebrations*. New York: Aladdin.

——. 1998. *The Table Where Rich People Sit*. New York: Aladdin Picture Books.

Bealle, Pamela and Susan Nipp. 2002. *Wee Sing, 25th Anniversary Celebration*. New York: Price, Stern, Sloane.

Berger, Melvin and Gilda Berger. 2001. *What Makes an Ocean Wave? Questions and Answers About Oceans and Ocean Life*. New York: Scholastic.

——. 2000. *Do Tarantulas Have Teeth? Questions and Answers About Poisonous Creatures*. New York: Scholastic.

——. 2000. *Why I Sneeze, Shiver, Hiccup, & Yawn*. New York: HarperTrophy.

Bernier-Grand, Carmen. 1995. *Juan Bobo—Four Folktales from Puerto Rico*. New York: HarperTrophy.

Bisal, Sara C. 1991. *The Secrets of Vesuvius*. New York: Scholastic.

Blake, Quentin. 1998. *Clown*. New York: Henry Holt & Co.

Boynton, Sandra. 1993. *Barnyard Dance*. New York: Workman Publishing.

——. 2004. *Rhinocerous TAP, The Book and the CD*. New York: Workman Publishing.

Branley, Franklyn. 1986. *What Makes Day and Night?* New York: HarperTrophy.

——. 1998. *The Planets in Our Solar System*. Let's-Read-and-Find-Out Science. New York: HarperTrophy.

——. 2000. *The International Space Station* (Let's-Read-and-Find-Out Science). New York: HarperTrophy.

Bridges, Shirin Yim. 2002. *Ruby's Wish*. San Francisco: Chronicle Books.

Briggs, Raymond. 2000. *The Snowman*. New York: Penguin.

Brown, Margaret Wise. 1989. *Big Red Barn*. New York: Scholastic.

Bruchac, Joseph. 1998. *A Boy Called Slow: The True Story of Sitting Bull*. New York: Putnam Publishing Group.

——. 1999. *Between Earth and Sky: Legends of Native American Sacred Places*. New York: Voyager Books.

——. 2000. *Crazy Horse's Vision*. New York: Lee & Low Books.

Buckley, James Jr. 2001. *MLB Home Run Heroes*, DK Readers Series. New York: DK Publishing, Inc.

Bunting, Eve. 1989. *The Wednesday Surprise*. Boston: Clarion Books.

——. 1990. *How Many Days to America?* Boston: Clarion Books.

——. 1999. *Night of the Gargoyles*. Boston: Clarion Books.

——. 1999. *Smoky Night*. New York: Voyager Books.

Cannon, Janell. 1993. *Stellaluna*. San Diego: Harcourt Children's Books.

Carling, Amelia Lau. 1998. *Mama and Papa Have a Store*. New York: Dial Books.

Carlson, Lori M., editor. 1995. *Cool Salsa: Poems on Growing Up Latino in the United States.* New York: Fawcett.

Castaneda, Omar S. 1995. *Abuela's Weave.* New York: Lee & Low Books.

Cha, Dia. 1996. *Dia's Story Cloth: The Hmong People's Journey of Freedom.* Denver: Museum of Natural History.

Chan, Jennifer. 1993. *One Small Girl.* Chicago: Polychrome Publishing.

Cherry, Lynne. 2000. *The Great Kapok Tree: A Tale of the Amazon Rain Forest.* New York: Voyager Books.

Chin-Lee, Cynthia. 1999. *A Is for Asia.* New York: Orchard Books.

Choi, Yangsook. 2003. *The Name Jar.* New York: Dragonfly Books.

Cisneros, Sandra. 1991. "Hairs." *The House on Mango Street.* New York: Vintage.

———. 1992. *Woman Hollering Creek and Other Stories.* New York: Vintage Books.

———. 1997. *Hairs/Pelitos.* New York: Dragonfly Books.

Cole, Joanna. 1989. *Hungry, Hungry Sharks.* New York: Random House.

———. 1989. *Magic School Bus: Inside the Earth.* New York: Scholastic.

———. 1992. *Magic School Bus: On the Ocean Floor.* New York: Scholastic.

"Columbus and the Taino." 2000. *A New Nation: Adventures in Time and Place.* New York: McGraw Hill.

Cowley, Joy. 1999. *Red-Eyed Tree Frog.* New York: Scholastic.

———. 2002. *Big Moon Tortilla.* Honesdale, PA: Boyds Mills Press.

Cox, Paul. 2001. *Abstract Alphabet.* New York: Chronicle Books.

Cronin, Doreen. 2000. *Click, Clack, Moo: Cows That Type.* New York: Simon & Schuster.

Dakos, Kalli. 2002. *The Bug in Teacher's Coffee: And Other School Poems.* New York: HarperTrophy.

Davies, Nicola. 2003. *Surprising Sharks.* Cambridge, MA: Candlewick Press

Day, Alexandra. 1997. *Good Dog, Carl!* New York: Aladdin.

———. 1998. *Follow Carl!* New York: Farrar, Straus and Giroux.

———. 2002. *Puppy Trouble* (pop-up version). New York: Farrar, Straus and Giroux.

dePaola, Tomie. 1990. *Pancakes for Breakfast.* New York: Voyager Books.

Delacre, Lulu. 2000. *Salsa Stories.* New York: Scholastic.

Demi, Hitz. 1982. *Liang and the Magic Paint Brush.* New York: Henry Holt & Co.

Dorros, Arthur. 1997. *Abuela.* New York: Puffin Books.

Dubowski, Mark. 1998. *Titanic: The Disaster That Shocked the World!* DK Readers Series. New York: Dorling Kindersley Publishing.

Dubowski, Mark and Cathy East Dubowski. 2001. *Ice Mummy: The Discovery of a 5,000-Year-Old Man.* Boston: Houghton Mifflin.

Endredy, James. 2003. *The Journey of the Tunuri and the Blue Deer: A Huichol Indian Story.* Rochester, VT: Bear Cub Books.

Filipovic, Zlata. 1995. *Zlata's Diary: A Child's Life in Sarajevo.* New York: Penguin Books.

Fleischmann, Paul. 1992. *Joyful Noise: Poems for Two Voices.* New York: HarperTrophy.

——. 1996. *Dateline: Troy.* Cambridge, MA: Candlewick Press.

Fleischman, Paul and Kevin Hawkes. 2004. *Sidewalk Circus.* Cambridge, MA: Candlewick Press.

Fleming, Candace. 2003. *Ben Franklin's Almanac, Being a True Account of the True Gentleman's Life.* New York: Atheneum.

Florian, Douglas. 1998. *beast feast: poems.* New York: Voyager Books.

——. 2001. *lizards, frogs, and polliwogs: poems and paintings.* San Diego: Harcourt Children's Books.

Frank, Anne. 1993. *Anne Frank: The Diary of a Young Girl.* New York: Bantam.

Freeman, Russell. 1996. *The Life and Death of Crazy Horse.* New York: Holiday House.

Friedman, Ina R. 1984. *How My Parents Learned to Eat.* Boston: Houghton Mifflin.

Ganeri, Anita. 1996. *How Would You Survive as an Ancient Roman?* New York: Franklin Watts/Grolier.

Garza, Carmen Lomas. 1990. *Family Pictures, Cuadros de familia.* San Francisco: Children's Book Press.

——. 2000. *In My Family, En mi familia.* San Francisco: Children's Book Press.

George, Jean Craighead. 1995. *One Day in the Tropical Rain Forest.* New York: HarperTrophy.

——. 1997. *Everglades.* New York: HarperTrophy.

——. 1998. *Look to the North: A Wolf Pup Diary.* New York: HarperTrophy.

George, Judith. 2000. *So You Want to Be President?* New York: Philomel Books.

Gerstein, Mordecai. 2003. *The Man Who Walked Between the Towers.* Brookfield, CT: Roaring Brook.

Gibbons, Gail. 1994. *The Planets.* New York: Holiday House.

——. 1995. *Wolves.* New York: Holiday House.

——. 1998. *The Moon Book.* New York: Holiday House.

——. 2000. *Bats.* New York: Holiday House.

Goebel, Nancy Andrews. 2002. *The Pot That Juan Built.* New York: Lee & Low Books.

Goffin, Josse. 2000. *Oh!* New York: Harry N. Abrams.

Gross, Ruth Belov. 1993. *. . . If You Grew Up With George Washington.* New York: Scholastic.

Guiberson, Brenda Z. 1993. *Cactus Hotel.* New York: Henry Holt & Co.

——. 2000. *Into the Sea.* New York: Henry Holt & Co.

Hakim, Joy. 2003. *War, Terrible War.* A History of Us, Book Six. Oxford, UK: Oxford University Press.

Harjo, Joy. 2000. *The Good Luck Cat.* New York: Harcourt Children's Books.

Hayden, Kate. 2000. *Twisters,* DK Readers Series. New York: DK Publishing.

Hayes, Joe. 1987. *La Llorona, The Weeping Woman.* El Paso, TX: Cinco Puntos Press.

Heard, Georgia. 1992. *Creatures of the Earth, Sea, and Sky: Poems.* Honesdale, PA: Boyds Mills Press.

Henkes, Kevin. 1988. *Chester's Way.* New York: Greenwillow Books.

——. 1990. *Julius, the Baby of the World.* New York: Greenwillow Books.

——. 1991. *Chrysanthemum.* New York: Greenwillow Books.

——. 1993. *Owen.* New York: Greenwillow Books.

——. 2000. *Wemberly Worried.* New York: Greenwillow Books.

Heo, Yumi. 1996. *The Green Frogs: A Korean Folktale.* Boston: Houghton Mifflin.

Herrera, Juan Felipe. 1998. *Laughing Out Loud, I Fly.* New York: Joanna Cotler (Harper Childrens).

——. 2000. *The Upside Down Boy.* San Francisco: Children's Book Press.

——. 2001. *Calling the Doves.* San Francisco: Children's Book Press.

——. 2002. *Grandma and Me at the Flea.* San Francisco: Children's Book Press.

Hill, Eric. 1980. *Where's Spot?* Lift the Flap Series. New York: Putnam Books.

Ho, Minfong. 1996. *Hush!* New York: Orchard Books.

——. 2004. *Peek! A Thai Hide-and-Seek.* Cambridge, MA: Candlewick Press.

Hoban, Tana. 1987. *Is it Red? Is It Yellow? Is It Blue?* New York: HarperTrophy.

Hodgson, Mona. 2004. *Bedtime in the Southwest.* Flagstaff, AZ: Rising Moon.

Hopkinson, Deborah. 1995. *Sweet Clara and the Freedom Quilt.* New York: Dragonfly Books.

Howker, Janni. 2002. *Walk with a Wolf.* Cambridge, MA: Candlewick Press.

Hutchins, Pat. 1992. *Rosie's Walk* (big book version). New York: Scholastic.

James, Simon. 2004. *Ancient Rome: Eyewitness Books.* New York: DK Children.

Jenkins, Steve. 2001. *What Do You Do When Something Wants to Eat You?* Boston: Houghton Mifflin.

——. 2003. *Looking Down.* Boston: Houghton Mifflin.

——. 2003. *What Do You Do With a Tail Like This?* Boston: Houghton Mifflin.

Jimenez, Francisco. 1997. *The Circuit: Stories from the Life of a Migrant Child.* Albuquerque: University of New Mexico Press.

——. 2000. *La Mariposa.* Boston: Houghton Mifflin.

Jones, Carol. 1998. *Old MacDonald Had a Farm.* Boston: Houghton Mifflin.

Kaner, Etta. 1999. *Animal Defenses: How Animals Protect Themselves.* Tonawanda, NY: Kids Can Press.

Katz, Karen. 1999. *The Color of Us.* New York: Henry Holt & Co.

Keats, Ezra Jack. 1999. *Clementina's Cactus.* New York: Viking Books.

Kerrod, Robin. 2002. *1,000 Questions and Answers.* Boston: Kingfisher.

Kotzwinkle, William. 2001. *The Return of Crazy Horse.* Berkeley, CA: North Atlantic Books.

Krull, Kathleen. 2003. *Harvesting Hope: The Story of Cesar Chavez.* San Diego: Harcourt.

Kyuchukov, Hristo. 2004. *My Name Was Hussein.* Honesdale, PA: Boyds Mills Books.

Lange, Karen E. 2002. "Wolf to Woof: Evolution of Dogs." *National Geographic* magazine, January. Washington, DC: National Geographic.

Lauber, Patricia. 1986. *Volcano.* New York: Simon & Schuster.

Lazaroff, David. 2001. *Correctamundo: Prickly Pete's Guide to Desert Facts & Cactifracts.* Tucson: Arizona–Sonoran Desert Museum Press.

Lee, Jeanne E. 1994. *Silent Lotus.* New York: Farrar, Straus and Giroux.

Levine, Ellen. 1993. *. . . If You Traveled on the Underground Railroad.* New York: Scholastic.

——. 1995. *I Hate English.* New York: Cartwheel Books.

Lewis, Richard. 2002. *In the Space of the Sky.* San Diego: Harcourt

Children's Books.

Lin, Grace. 2001. *Dim Sum for Everyone*. New York: Knopf Books.

——. 2001. *The Ugly Vegetables*. Watertown, MA: Charlesbridge Publishing.

——. 2004. *Fortune Cookie Fortunes*. New York: Knopf Books.

Ling, Mary and Mary Atkinson. 2000. *The Snake Book, A Breathtaking Close-Up Look at Splendid, Scaly, Slithery Snakes*. New York: DK Publishing.

Lipp, Frederick. 2000. *The Caged Birds of Phnom Penh*. New York: Holiday House.

——. 2004. *Bread Song*. New York: Mondo.

Lithgow, John. 2004. Saint Saens's *Carnival of the Animals* (with CD). New York: Simon & Schuster Books for Young Readers.

Lobel, Arnold. 1983. *Fables*. New York: HarperTrophy.

London, Jonathon. 2000. *Panther, Shadow of the Swamp*. Cambridge, MA: Candlewick Press.

Look, Lenore. 1999. *Love as Strong as Ginger*. New York: Atheneum.

——. 2001. *Henry's First-Moon Birthday*. New York: Atheneum.

——. 2004. *Ruby Lu, Brave and True*. New York: Atheneum.

Lowell, Susan. 1992. *The Three Little Javelinas*. Flagstaff, AZ: Rising Moon Books.

Luthardt, Kevin. 2003. *Peep!* Atlanta: Peachtree Press.

Maizlish, Lisa. 1996. *The Ring*. New York: Greenwillow Books.

Malone, Peter and Janet Schulman. 2004. Sergei Prokofiev's *Peter and the Wolf* (with CD). New York: Alfred A. Knopf.

Marshall, James. 1974. *George and Martha Back in Town*. Boston: Houghton Mifflin.

——. 1977. *George and Martha Encore*. Boston: Houghton Mifflin.

——. 1986. *George and Martha Tons of Fun*. Boston: Houghton Mifflin.

——. 1991. *George and Martha Round and Round*. Boston: Houghton Mifflin.

——. 1997. *George and Martha: The Complete Stories of Two Best Friends*. Boston: Houghton Mifflin.

Martin, Bill and Eric Carle. 1996. *Brown Bear, Brown Bear, What Do You See?* New York: Henry Holt & Co.

McCauley, David. 1998. *The New Way Things Work*. Boston: Houghton Mifflin.

McCully, Emily Arnold. 2001. *Four Hungry Kittens*. New York: Dial Books for Young Readers.

Medina, Jane. 1999. *My Name is Jorge: On Both Sides of the River, Poems in English and Spanish*. Honesdale, PA: Boyds Mills Press.

Miles, Miska. 1985. *Annie and the Old One*. New York: Little, Brown.

Mochizuki, Ken. 1995. *Baseball Saved Us*. New York: Lee & Low Books.

Montes, Marisa. 2000. *Juan Bobo Goes to Work: A Puerto Rican Folktale*. New York: HarperCollins.

Mora, Pat. 1994. *Pablo's Tree*. New York: Simon & Schuster.

——. 1997. *A Birthday Basket for Tia*. New York: Aladdin Picture Books.

——. 1999. *Confetti: Poems for Children*. New York: Lee & Low Books.

——. 2000. *Tomás and the Library Lady*. New York: Dragonfly Books.

Morales, Yuyi. 2003. *Just a Minute: a Trickster Tale and Counting Book*. San Francisco: Chronicle Books.

Morris, Ann. 1993. *Bread, Bread, Bread*. New York: HarperTrophy.

——. 1993. *Hats, Hats, Hats*. New York: HarperTrophy.

——. 1994. *On the Go*. New York: HarperTrophy.

——. 1998. *Shoes, Shoes, Shoes*. New York: HarperTrophy.

——. 1998. *Tools*. New York: HarperTrophy.

——. 1998. *Work*. New York: HarperCollins.

——. 2000. *Families*. New York: HarperCollins.

Most, Bernard. 2003. *The Cow That Went Oink*. New York: Voyager Books.

Murphy, Jim. 1993. *The Boys' War: Confederate and Union Soldiers Talk About the Civil War*. Boston: Clarion Books.

Myers, Christopher. 2000. *Wings*. New York: Scholastic.

——. 2001. *Fly*. New York: Jump at the Sun.

Nicholson, Sue. 1998. *A Day at Greenhill Farm*. New York: DK Publishing.

Nye, Naomi Shihab. 1997. *Sitti's Secrets*. New York: Aladdin Picture Books.

——. 2000. *Come With Me: Poems for a Journey*. New York: Greenwillow Books.

Nye, Naomi Shihab, ed. 2000. *Salting the Ocean: 100 Poems by Young Poets*. New York: Greenwillow Books.

Osborne, Mary Pope. 2003. *Dolphins and Sharks: Magic Tree House Research Guide*. New York: Random House Books for Young Readers.

——. 2004. *Magic Tree House Research Guides: Ancient Greece and the Olympics*. New York: Random House Books for Young Readers.

Page, Robin and Steve Jenkins. 2003. *What Do You Do With a Tail Like This?* Boston: Houghton Mifflin.

Park, Frances and Ginger Park. 1998. *My Freedom Trip: A Child's Escape from North Korea.* Honesdale, PA: Boyds Mills Press.

——. 2000. *The Royal Bee.* Honesdale, PA: Boyds Mills Press.

Park, Linda Sue. 2000. *Kite Fighters.* Boston: Clarion Books.

——. 2004. *The Firekeeper's Son.* Boston: Clarion Books.

Perez, Amada Irma. 2000. *My Very Own Room.* San Francisco: Children's Book Press.

——. 2002. *My Diary From Here to There.* San Francisco: Children's Book Press.

Perez, L. King. 2002. *First Day in Grapes.* New York: Lee & Low Books.

Perkins, Lynn Rae. 2003. *Snow Music.* New York: Greenwillow Books.

"Plants of the Rain Forests." 1997. *Rain Forests, Kids Discover* magazine. Boulder, CO: Kids Discover.

Platt, Richard. 2002. *Spiders' Secrets,* DK Readers Series. New York: DK Publishing.

Polacco, Patricia. 1997. *Thunder Cake.* New York: PaperStar Books.

——. 1998. *Chicken Sunday.* New York: PaperStar Books.

——. 1998. *My Rotten, Redheaded Older Brother.* New York: Aladdin.

——. 2000. *The Butterfly.* New York: Philomel.

——. 2001. *Mrs. Katz and Tush.* New York: Dragonfly Books.

——. 2001. *Mrs. Mack.* New York: Putnam.

——. 2001. *Thank You, Mr. Falker.* New York: Philomel.

——. 2001. *The Keeping Quilt.* New York: Aladdin.

Popov, Nikolai. 1998. *Why?* New York: Michael Neugebauer.

Radley, Gail. 2001. *Vanishing From Waterways: Poems.* Minneapolis: Carolrhoda Books.

Ramírez, Antonio. 2004. *Napí.* Toronto: Douglas & McIntyre.

Ramirez, Michael Rose. 1998. *The Legend of the Hummingbird: A Tale from Puerto Rico.* New York: Mondo.

Rappaport, Doreen. 2001. *Martin's Big Words.* New York: Scholastic.

Rattigan, Jama Kim. 1998. *Dumpling Soup.* New York: Megan Tingley.

Recorvitz, Helen. 2003. *My Name Is Yoon.* Farrar, Straus and Giroux.

Ringgold, Faith. 1995. *Aunt Harriet's Underground Railroad in the Sky.* New York: Dragonfly Books.

Ripley, Catherine. 2001. *Why?: The Best Ever Question and Answer Book About Nature, Science and the World Around You.* Toronto: Maple Tree Press.

Rohmann, Eric. 1997. *Time Flies.* New York: Dragonfly Books.

——. 2002. *My Friend Rabbit.* New York: Scholastic.

Ryan, Pam Munoz. 2001. *Mice and Beans.* New York: Scholastic.

Ryder, Joanne. 1999. *Tyrannosaurus Time* (Just for a Day book). New York: Morrow Junior Books.

Rylant, Cynthia. 1988. *Every Living Thing.* New York: Aladdin Paperbacks.

Rylant, Cynthia and Walker Evans. 1994. *Something Permanent.* San Diego: Harcourt, Brace & Co.

Saenz, Benjamin Alire. 1998. *A Gift from Papá Diego.* El Paso, TX: Cinco Puntos Press.

——. 2001. *Grandma Fina and Her Wonderful Umbrellas.* El Paso, TX: Cinco Puntos Press.

Scieszka, John. 1989. *The True Story of the Three Little Pigs!* New York: Putnam.

——. 1991. *The Frog Prince Continued.* New York: Puffin Books.

——. 1992. *The Stinky Cheese Man and Other Fairly Stupid Tales.* New York: Viking.

Settel, Joanne. 1999. *Exploding Ants: Amazing Facts About How Animals Adapt.* New York: Atheneum.

Shea, Peggy Deitz. 1996. *The Whispering Cloth: A Refugee's Story.* Honesdale, PA: Boyds Mills Press.

Simon, Seymour. 1995. *Wolves.* New York: HarperTrophy.

——. 2002. *Animals Nobody Loves.* New York: SeaStar Books.

Sis, Peter. 2000. *An Ocean World.* New York: HarperTrophy.

——. 2000. *Dinosaur!* New York: Greenwillow Books.

Smith, Cynthia Leitich. 2000. *Jingle Dancer.* New York: Morrow Junior Books.

Smith, Jerry. 1991. *Who Says Quack?* New York: Grosset & Dunlap.

Soto, Gary. 1991. *A Summer Life.* New York: Laurel Leaf (Random House).

——. 1994. *Neighborhood Odes.* New York: Scholastic.

——. 1996. *Too Many Tamales.* New York: Putnam Publishing Group.

——. 1997. *Chato's Kitchen.* New York: PaperStar Books (Putnam Publishing Group).

——. 1998. *Snapshots from the Wedding.* New York: Putnam Publishing Group.

——. 1998. *The Old Man and His Door.* New York: Putnam Publishing Group.

——. 2000. *Chato and the Party Animals.* New York: Putnam Publishing Group.

Spagnoli, Cathy and Lina Mao Wall. 1992. *Judge Rabbit and the Tree Spirit: A Folktale from Cambodia*. San Francisco: Children's Book Press.

St. John, Victoria. 2001. *Dolphins*. Bothell, WA: Wright Group/McGraw-Hill.

Stanchak, John. 2000. *Civil War: Eyewitness Books*. New York: DK Publishers.

Stavans, Ilan, editor. 2001. *Wáchale: Poetry and Prose About Growing Up Latino in America*. Chicago: Cricket Books (Carus Publishing Co.).

Steig, William. 1990. *Dr. De Soto*. New York: Farrar, Straus and Giroux.

——. 1992. *Amos and Boris*. New York: Farrar, Straus and Giroux.

——. 1993. *Shrek!* New York: Farrar, Straus and Giroux.

Stevens, Janet. 2001. *And the Dish Ran Away With the Spoon*. San Diego: Harcourt.

Surat, Michele. 1989. *Angel Child, Dragon Child*. New York: Scholastic.

Swartz, Stanley L. 1999. *Sea Turtles*. Carlsbad, CA: Dominie Press, Inc.

Taback, Simms. 1997. *There Was an Old Lady Who Swallowed a Fly*. New York: Viking Books.

——. 1999. *Joseph Had a Little Overcoat*. New York: Viking Children's Books.

——. 2002. *This Is the House That Jack Built*. New York: G. P. Putnam Sons.

Tafuri, Nancy. 1991. *Have You Seen My Duckling?* New York: HarperTrophy.

Tan, Amy. 1995. *The Moon Lady*. New York: Aladdin Picture Books.

——. 2001. *Sagawa, The Chinese Siamese Cat*. New York: Aladdin.

Thong, Roseanne. 2000. *Round Is a Mooncake: A Book of Shapes*. San Francisco: Chronicle Books.

——. 2001. *Red Is a Dragon: A Book of Colors*. San Francisco: Chronicle Books.

Time-Life Books. 1992. *Pompeii: The Vanished City*. New York.

Tokuda, Wendy and Richard Hall. 1992. *Humphrey, The Lost Whale, a True Story*. Torrance, CA: Heian.

Uchida, Yoshiko. 1996. *The Bracelet*. New York: Putnam Publishing Group.

Van Allsburg, Chris. 1981. *Jumanji*. Boston: Houghton Mifflin.

——. 1983. *The Wreck of the Zephyr*. Boston: Houghton Mifflin.

——. 1984. *The Mysteries of Harris Burdick*. Boston: Houghton Mifflin.

——. 1985. *The Polar Express*. Boston: Houghton Mifflin.

——. 1986. *The Stranger*. Boston: Houghton Mifflin.

——. 1988. *Two Bad Ants.* Boston: Houghton Mifflin.

——. 1990. *Just a Dream.* Boston: Houghton Mifflin.

Vincent, Gabrielle. 2000. *A Day, A Dog.* Honesdale, PA: Front Street.

Wallace, Karen. 2001. *Diving Dolphins,* DK Readers Series. New York: DK Publishing.

——. 2001. *Rockets and Spaceships,* DK Readers Series. New York: DK Publishing.

Waterlow, Julia. 1998. *Family from Bosnia.* Austin, TX: Raintree.

Weisner, David. 1991. *Free Fall.* Boston: Clarion Books.

——. 1995. *June 29, 1999.* Boston: Clarion Books.

——. 1997. *Tuesday.* Boston: Clarion Books.

——. 1999. *Sector 7.* Boston: Clarion Books.

Weitzman, Jacqueline. 2000. *You Can't Take a Balloon into the National Gallery.* New York: Dial Books.

Wells, Rosemary. 2001. *Yoko's Paper Cranes.* New York: Hyperion Books for Children.

Wick, Walter. 1995. *I Spy School Days: A Book of Picture Riddles.* New York: Scholastic.

——. 1999. *I Spy Treasure Hunt: A Book of Picture Riddles* (I Spy books). New York: Scholastic.

——. 2002. *Can You See What I See?* (I Spy books). New York: Scholastic.

Willems, Mo. 2003. *Don't Let the Pigeon Ride the Bus!* New York: Hyperion Press.

Wilson, April. 1999. *Magpie Magic: A Tale of Colorful Mischief.* New York. Dial Books.

Wilson, Karma. 2003. *Bear Wants More.* New York: Margaret K. McElderry.

Winter, Jeanette. 1992. *Follow the Drinking Gourd.* New York: Dragonfly Books.

Wong, Janet. 1996. *A Suitcase of Seaweed and Other Poems.* New York: Margaret K. McElderry.

——. 2000. *The Trip Back Home.* San Diego: Harcourt Children's Books.

——. 2002. *Apple Pie 4th of July.* San Diego: Harcourt Children's Books.

——. 2002. *Buzz.* New York: Voyager.

Wood, Don and Audrey Wood. 1984. *The Little Mouse, the Red, Ripe Strawberry, and the Big Hungry Bear.* Wiltshire, UK: Child's Play (International) Ltd.

Wood, Douglas. 2003. *Old Turtle and the Broken Truth.* New York: Scholastic.

Worth, Valerie. 1996. *all the small poems and fourteen more*. New York: Farrar, Straus and Giroux.

Wright-Frierson, Virginia. 1996. *A Desert Scrapbook: Dawn to Dusk in the Sonoran Desert*. New York: Simon & Schuster.

———. 1998. *An Island Scrapbook: Dawn to Dusk on a Barrier Island*. New York: Simon & Schuster.

———. 2003. *A North American Rain Forest Scrapbook*. New York: Walker & Company.

Xiong, Blia and Cathy Spagnoli. 1989. *Nine-in-One, Grr! Grr! A Folktale from the Hmong People of Laos*. San Francisco: Children's Book Press.

Yep, Lawrence. 1996. *Hiroshima*. New York: Scholastic.

Yin. 2001. *Coolies*. New York: Puffin Books.

Yolen, Jane. 1992. *Encounter*. San Diego: Harcourt Brace.

———. 1996. *Sky Scrape/City Scape, Poems of City Life*. Honesdale, PA: Boyds Mills Press.

———. 2003. *How Do Dinosaurs Get Well Soon?* New York: Blue Sky Press.

Zelinsky, Paul. 1990. *The Wheels on the Bus*. New York: Dutton Children's Books.

Zoehfeld, Kathleen Weidner. 1994. *What Lives in a Shell?* New York: HarperTrophy.

———. 1995. *How Mountains Are Made*. New York: HarperTrophy.

———. 2003. *Dolphin's First Day: The Story of a Bottlenose Dolphin* (Smithsonian Oceanic Collection). Norwalk, CT: Soundprints.

APPENDIX

Judge Rabbit and the Snail Race

One day, Judge Rabbit was thirsty and wanted a drink.
He went to a lake where there were many snails in the water.

When he was about to drink the lake water, a snail came up and asked, "Hey Rabbit, I heard someone say that you run very fast. Is that true?"

Judge Rabbit responded proudly, "That's true."
Of all the animals who have legs, none of them run as fast as I do. I am the fastest one of all."

The snail decided to play a trick on Judge Rabbit, so he said, "If you are the fastest animal of all, why don't you race with me? Let's make a bet. If I win, you cannot drink this water, but if you win, I will leave the lake."

Judge Rabbit was surprised. "What a silly idea you have!" he exclaimed. "It is a big mistake to dare me to race."

The snail answered, "Are you afraid of me? Let's race around the lake, and we will see who is faster!" They agreed to meet the next morning.

After the rabbit left, the snail gathered his friends together. "Friends, you all know that we can't even run as fast as the caterpillar, let alone the rabbit, but listen carefully. We will all disperse along the shore of the lake. When the rabbit calls, 'Snail, where are you?' The one of you in front of him must answer, 'I'm here.'"

The next morning the snails spread out all around the big lake. As the time for the race drew near, Judge Rabbit appeared. "What are we waiting for?" the original snail challenged. "Are you afraid?"

Judge Rabbit did not know that the snails would play a trick on him. "Who in the world would be afraid of you, Snail?" he answered angrily. "Then, let's go!" the snail replied.

In this way, the race started.

After a few minutes, Judge Rabbit turned around looking for the snail. He called out, "Snail, where are you?" and as the snails had planned, the snail in front of him answered, "I'm here!"

This surprised Judge Rabbit and he sped up. He called again, "Snail, where are you?"

Judge Rabbit ran as fast as he could, and as he continued around the lake, he cried out loudly, "Snail, where are you?"

Each time that he called, the snail in front of him would answer, "I'm here!"

Judge Rabbit continued running until he ran out of breath. When he stopped, the snail in front of him said, "Now, Brother Rabbit, remember the bet we made. Since you lost the race, from now on, you must not drink any of the lake water." So, Judge Rabbit promised not to come to the lake anymore.

This is the story about why rabbits only drink dew water.